Impromptu
WEEKENDS

IN THE UK

Impromptu
WEEKENDS

IN THE UK

FOR WHEN YOU JUST WANT TO GET UP AND GO

ROBIN NEILLANDS

Good Books

In association with

PUBLISHED IN ASSOCIATION WITH VOLVO CAR UK LIMITED

BY GOOD BOOKS (GB PUBLICATIONS LIMITED)

LAGARD FARM, WHITLEY, NR MELKSHAM, WILTS SN12 8RL

ISBN 0 946555 31 1

COVER AND INSIDE ILLUSTRATIONS BY JACK PENNINGTON

DESIGNED BY DESIGN/SECTION, FROME

PRINTED AND BOUND IN ENGLAND BY COX & WYMAN, READING

HOTEL, RESTAURANT AND TIC DETAILS WERE CORRECT AT

THE TIME OF GOING TO PRINT.

Contents

—

A Message from Volvo

Some months ago, the thought of a guide to the perfect 'impromptu' weekend away was most attractive.

As the book has taken shape, we have been delighted to see that not only does the 'get up and go' concept work really well, but it's been great fun getting there!

We have discovered the universal attraction of the last-minute decision...an unplanned, impromptu visit to an idyllic and largely unexplored retreat in the UK is the ultimate weekend away.

And we did, of course, have our discerning Volvo customers in mind - looking for the stylish, the unusual, the individual options.

Whatever time of year and whatever the occasion, we hope this guide will become a valuable source of information and a must for every bookshelf.

VOLVO CAR UK LIMITED

INTRODUCTION

This book is a collection of ideas for leisurely weekend breaks in some of the most delightful corners of Britain. The towns and areas suggested range from Dartmoor in the far south-west of England north to the Scottish Highlands, east from Tenby in Pembrokeshire to the coastal resort of Southwold in Suffolk. Wherever you live, there will be somewhere worth visiting within easy reach.

Many of the areas chosen lie just that bit off the too-well-beaten track, and are all the better for it. The book features little known places like Otmoor, the Eden Valley, Strathmore, Pendle, the Cowal Peninsula and Pembroke, as well as more familiar spots like the Lake District, South Downs and Dedham Vale, though even here we have come up with a few surprises.

Most of the weekends are based in or near a town, which, importantly, provides visitors with somewhere to go if the weather is too foul for outdoor activities. That said, all these places have a great deal to offer in every season of the year and will give the visitor, whatever their tastes and interests, an enjoyable and interesting weekend break.

Knowing just where to go and what to see makes a major contribution to the success of any weekend, where time is necessarily limited. This book has drawn heavily on the advice of local people and the ever-helpful staff of the local Tourist Information Centres (TICs). We would urge all visitors to do the same.

These impromptu weekends offer those who take them the precious benefits of variety. Opportunities for walking, horse-riding, golf, fishing, birdwatching, visiting museums and historic sites, car touring or - for the less energetic - special shopping and even beauty treatments, abound throughout the book. The aim is to introduce the visitor to not only the main but also the lesser known attractions of each area, in the space of a few days. There is advice on the best routes to follow, pubs to visit, views to see, walks to take, gardens or stately homes to explore and enjoy. There are steam train rides and boat trips, hidden-away county corners to discover, battlefields and historic places to recall the past and inform the present. Above all, these weekends will be fun.

Nowhere listed should be more than a two-hour drive from a major population centre: London, Bristol, Cardiff, Birmingham, Leeds, Manchester, Newcastle, Edinburgh, Glasgow... From cities like these, places such as the Peak District, Exmoor, the Scottish borders, the Forest of Dean, the Northern Lakes or Pennines, or historic towns like Sandwich, Beverley, Sherborne, Stamford or Lincoln, are within easy reach on a Friday evening. The book gives the approximate mileages to each destination rather than the time required; journey times are difficult to estimate in these days of traffic jams and road repairs, and readers are advised to obtain precise directions to each place when booking their hotel.

For each weekend break we have suggested one or two suitable hotels. All offer good food and comfortable accommodation and some feature that makes them particularly right for the proposed weekend or area. Most of them are country house hotels or former coaching inns. All of them are well-run, friendly and hospitable establishments with a certain atmosphere and style.

Such assets do not come cheap, but all of these hotels offer excellent value for money and the bonus of weekend rates. Prices can be obtained before booking and a further selection of accommodation can be acquired from the local TIC, the telephone number of which is given for every locale.

Read this book; choose an area, a hotel, places you and yours want to see and things you would like to do. Fling a few items into a weekend bag, not forgetting the boots, the bike, the swimsuit, the golf clubs or the fishing rod; and of course this book. Then get up and go - and have a great weekend.

Alnwick and the Northumbrian Coast

The Northumbrian Tourist Board used to refer to Northumbria as 'Britain's best kept secret'. This was perfectly true for Northumbria is a place that people tend to pass through, rushing to Scotland or Yorkshire, with barely a glance at the attractions on either side of the A1.

Northumbria is also very big, taking in three counties and offering a great variety of interesting things to see or do. For this weekend I have chosen the Northumbrian coast, north of the fine town of Alnwick.

Alnwick is 80 miles from Edinburgh, 120 miles from Glasgow, and 129 miles from Leeds.

Alnwick is the touring centre for the Northumbrian coast with the main attractions lying just to the north, between Alnwick and Berwick-on-Tweed; but no one should leave Alnwick - which is pronounced 'Annick' - without first having a good look around this historic town. Alnwick was built to bar the eastern road into England against the Scots. Since the early Middle Ages it has been the seat of the Percies, Earls and Dukes of Northumberland, whose descendants still live in Alnwick Castle. The stamp of the Percies can be seen all over Alnwick. One of the first sights which greets the eye is the stiff-tailed Percy Lion standing high on the pillar of the Percy Tenantry Column, erected in 1818 in gratitude to the 2nd Duke for lowering rents during the Napoleonic Wars. Nearby stands another, much older memorial, the Percy - or Hotspur - Tower, the last of the medieval gateways in the walls which once surrounded the town. Within the line of the long-gone walls are a number of streets called 'gates' - Bondgate, Canongate, Pottergate, Bailiffgate - all of which once led through the walls. Bailiffgate leads to Alnwick Castle, a splendid pile where one of the curious features is the number of small figures of men-at-arms, dotted about on the towers and battlements. Close to, they simply look odd, but in former times they appeared to be soldiers of a strong and alert garrison, and on seeing them any raiding Scot would promptly go home. Or so it is said.

Alnwick Castle was built in the 11th century and although the present building was much restored in the 18th century, it remains as a fine example of a medieval fortress. Lovers of medieval castles will appreciate the fabric of Alnwick, but the inside of the castle is no less attractive. The state rooms and library are full of treasures, including pictures by Canaletto, Van Dyck and Titian, as well as fine furniture and a great quantity of antiques. Hulne Park, surrounding the castle, was landscaped by Capability Brown, himself a Northumbrian, and from the Brizlee Tower in the park it is possible to see the outlines of no less than seven other castles.

After touring the castle, it is time to explore the town. One of the more curious attractions is a pub called Ye Olde Crosse. This pub takes its name from the cross carved in the stonework, but the local people call it 'The Dirty Bottles', from the small pile of dirty and cobwebbed bottles displayed in the pub window.

These have been there for nearly 200 years and are likely to remain there, for they are said to be cursed. The man who put the bottles in the window fell down and died shortly afterwards, declaring that anyone who moved or touched them would suffer a similar fate; there they still are, and no one in Alnwick would dream of laying a finger on them.

The centre of old Alnwick is the market square, with its Market Cross. This square reverts to its old self in June when the town stages a week-long costumed medieval pageant. Nearby is the White Swan Hotel on Bondgate Within. This is a coaching inn, dating from 1729, and a very comfortable hostelry with one singular feature, the Olympic Suite, taken intact from the SS *Olympic*, sister ship of the ill-fated *Titanic*.

Among the town's other attractions are Barter Books at Alnwick Station, which is one of the largest secondhand bookshops in the north with more than 30,000 volumes on sale at any time, and the House of

Hardy's fishing tackle shop, factory and museum on the south side of the town.

It would be quite possible to spend an entire weekend exploring Alnwick, but the coastline beckons.

My suggestion is to begin at Warkworth, seven miles to the south, for the castle here was the home of that famous knight, Harry Hotspur, a scion of the Percies, who owned Warkworth for over 600 years. The castle now belongs to English Heritage and is a beautiful building in mellow golden stone. There is a good short walk from here along the River Coquet for half a mile to the hermitage at Warkworth, and the fortified gatehouse by the bridge is another attraction. Somewhere else well worth a trip, especially for birdwatchers, is Coquet Island, an RSPB reserve a mile offshore which can be visited by boat from the tiny harbour at Amble.

After Warkworth, head north along the coast to another little port, Craster. Craster is famous for herrings, or in their smoked form, kippers, and lies in the centre of an AONB (Area of Outstanding Natural Beauty). The harbour at Craster dates from the turn of the century but the two principal features of this little port are the 'kipper teas' on sale by the quay, and the one-mile walk north along the coast to the ruins of Dunstanburgh Castle.

South of Craster another short walk takes you to Howick Hall, which has belonged to another local family, the Greys, since 1319. The gardens of Howick Hall are magnificent in the spring when the rhododendrons and azaleas are in bloom, but worth a visit at any time.

Heading north from Craster a minor road leads to the port of Seahouses and the village and castle of Bamburgh. On the way note the flat rocks of the Farne Islands, now a bird sanctuary. The Farnes can be visited by boat from Seahouses. The round trip, with time to watch the seabirds, takes about two hours, but landing on the Farnes is restricted, particularly during the nesting season, and can be wet work if any sea is running.

The Farne Islands provided the setting for the epic story of Grace Darling, a young girl from Bamburgh who became a national heroine in

1838 when she and her father set out one dark and stormy night to rescue the crew of the SS *Forfarshire*, driven onto the Farne Rocks during a gale. Her story is recalled in the Grace Darling Museum at Bamburgh.

Bamburgh Castle is one of the finest castles in England, a vast bastion set on a cliff above the sea, glaring towards Scotland and across the seascapes to one of the other famous places on this fascinating coast, Lindisfarne, the Holy Island.

Lindisfarne is only a part-time island and when the tide is out is connected to the mainland by a causeway. The island is a place of

Lindisfarne Castle, Holy Isle

pilgrimage, and has been since St Aiden came here in AD635. Aiden was followed by St Cuthbert and after Cuthbert's death another monk, Eadfrith, completed the illustrated manuscripts known as the Lindisfarne Gospels. The originals are now in the British Museum but the 12th-century church of St Mary's, alongside the melancholy ruins of Lindisfarne Priory, has some excellent reproductions.

Lindisfarne is full of attractions, including seals and a prolific birdlife, but the most dramatic sight is Lindisfarne Castle, on a sharp spur of rock at the seaward end. The castle was built in the reign of Henry VIII and eventually became the home of Sir Edwin Lutyens. It now belongs to the National Trust. Take as much time as possible to explore Lindisfarne but keep an eye on the clock, for once the tide comes in visitors will have to stay on the island for another 12 hours.

There is much more to do around Northumbria, but those who begin with Alnwick and a tour along the coast will have made a good start, and whetted their appetites for another visit.

INFORMATION:

ALNWICK LIES BESIDE THE A1, MIDWAY BETWEEN NEWCASTLE-UPON-TYNE AND BERWICK-UPON-TWEED.

WHITE SWAN HOTEL, ALNWICK, TEL. 0665 602109; BAMBURGH CASTLE HOTEL, SEAHOUSES, TEL. 0665 720283. TIC (ALNWICK), TEL. 0665 510665/510450.

2

Appleby and the Northern Pennines

—

The Pennines are the backbone of England, running from the Derbyshire Peaks to the Scottish border, and provide the backdrop to this weekend around Appleby-in-Westmorland, in the country east of the Lake District.

This is another little-visited part of England, beautiful at any time of the year. The attractive small town of Appleby sits astride the River Eden. There are plenty of places to visit in the area, with lots of scope for walking, horse-riding and mountain-biking in the surrounding hills.

Appleby is 70 miles from Newcastle, 90 miles from Leeds, 110 miles from Manchester, and 130 miles from Edinburgh.

As the centre for this weekend in the Vale of Eden I have chosen the town of Appleby-in-Westmorland. The county of Westmorland no longer exists, though there are hopes of a revival, but up to 1974, Appleby was the county town. Appleby is a very old town, gaining a charter for a market in 1174, a pleasant place set into a loop of the River Eden, with a castle on the hill at the top end and the church of St Lawrence at the bottom of Boroughgate.

The castle predates the town and went up round about 1100. It eventually fell into the hands of the Cliffords, who were great landowners in the north of England, and they held Appleby Castle until the Civil War, when Cromwell's cannon knocked it to pieces.

Much of the castle was rebuilt by the remarkable Lady Anne Clifford after the war ended, and the Great Hall still contains a triptych showing Lady Anne and members of her family. The castle and grounds now house a Conservation Centre, which devotes itself to the preservation of rare farm animals and some wild birds.

The centre has on display rare breeds of pigs, goats and cattle as well as owls, ravens, flamingoes and other birds, while the 25 acres of grounds surrounding the castle include, among other attractions, a two-mile-long nature trail.

Appleby is famous for the annual Horse Fair, held during the second week in June, when gypsies and horse brokers flock here from all over Britain and Ireland. The horses are bathed in the Eden and show off their paces in gallops up the main street, while the town is packed with colourful people and even more colourful caravans. The pubs, especially the 17th-century A'board Inn, halfway down Boroughgate, do a roaring trade.

Another, more permanent attraction, is the almshouses of St Anne's Hospital in Boroughgate, built by Lady Anne Clifford in the 1650s and still providing a home for the town's widows.

There are good walks from the town along the banks of the Eden and serious walking in the Pennine Hills, which are in plain sight a few miles away to the east, with various trails like the Maiden Way leading up from the valley floor towards the Lune Forest and the Pennine Way.

Appleby has several good hotels, each with something special to offer. The Tufton Arms Hotel in the market square was the RAC Hotel of the Year in 1991-2 and has won many other awards, while offering guests the useful extra of access to 24 miles of fly fishing. Appleby Manor is a resort hotel where the

Appleby's Horse Fair - trotting races

attractions include a steam room, jacuzzi and sauna, and an amazing collection of single malts.

The local attractions of Appleby itself, the golf courses, the fishing and the Saturday Market, would probably keep most people content for a weekend, but this is wonderful country for walking, bike-riding, pony-trekking or car touring, with scenery that simply begs to be seen.

The hanging hills of the Pennines are an irresistible lure and can be seen at their best on a tour north on the B6277 from Barnard Castle, 25 miles from Appleby down the A66. The latter is a very scenic road, leading to the town of Brough, which has a splendid ruined castle set against the backdrop of the Pennines.

Brough Castle was the stronghold of 'Bloody Clifford', a Lancastrian protagonist during the Wars of the Roses who appears in Shakespeare's *Henry VI* and came to a very nasty end at the battle of Towton. From the battlements of Brough Castle there are great views across the Eden Valley.

Barnard Castle is a market town with several good pubs along the main street, and a castle which guards the entrance to Teesdale. The B6277 through Teesdale is one of the most attractive roads in England, arrowing north through the Pennines, climbing steadily for 25 miles from Barnard Castle to Alston, the highest market town in England.

This short distance need take no more than an hour but wise visitors will allow at least half a day, for there are numerous diversions en route, not least the walk along the River Lune or to the High Force waterfall by the village of Newbiggin. The Pennine Way comes in to run beside the road near Alston, a very breezy spot, standing at the 1,000ft (305m) level, a jumbled little town with steeply sloping streets.

From Alston railway station there are trips through the North Pennines on the South Tyndale Railway. The trips last less than an hour but are a marvellous way to see the countryside.

From Alston take the A686 road west over and down the side of the Pennines to the town of Penrith, the northern gateway to the Lakes and the Vale of Eden. Penrith is a blunt workaday northern town, with few frills but some pleasing architecture.

Attractions in the town include the ruins of Penrith Castle, good shops, pubs and restaurants, and a very helpful and well-equipped Tourist Information Centre full of maps, books and leaflets. Next to the TIC stands the Penrith Museum, a good place to learn about life in the area.

Among local sights is the home of Lord and Lady Inglewood at Hutton-in-the-Forest, six miles north of Penrith on the B5305. This battlemented house stands in a park and gardens with hosts of daffodils in springtime, topiary on the terraces, and good walks in the grounds.

From Penrith it is a short ride back down the A66 to Appleby, but stop on the way at Temple Sowerby, to visit the herb garden at Acorn Bank. This is a National Trust property with a walled garden containing over 250 different kinds of medicinal and culinary herbs. Driving around this part of the Pennines will take a full day, but there is one other attraction no visitor should miss.

This is the famous Settle-to-Carlisle Railway, which is under constant threat of closure because the cost of maintaining the viaducts, bridges and track far exceeds the annual revenue. The Settle-to-Carlisle is a relic of the great age of railway engineers and as such a piece of industrial heritage, but the real fascination of this line is the wild and wonderful country through which it travels.

The Settle-to-Carlisle trains stop at Appleby, so travel on it now, while you still can: north for a day in Carlisle, or south across the moors for spectacular glimpses of the Northern Pennines.

INFORMATION:

APPLEBY-IN-WESTMORLAND LIES ON THE A66 BETWEEN PENRITH AND BARNARD CASTLE.

APPLEBY MANOR HOTEL, APPLEBY, TEL. 07683 51571; THE TUFTON ARMS HOTEL, APPLEBY, TEL. 07683 51593. TIC (APPLEBY), TEL. 07683 51177.

3

Beverley and the Yorkshire Wolds

—

Ask travellers about the country joys of Yorkshire and they will lead with the charms of the Moors and Dales. These are indeed splendid places but Yorkshire, however sub-divided or renamed - and this part of Yorkshire is officially North Humberside - contains many areas which are no less attractive for being less well known.

Among these are the Yorkshire Wolds; beautiful, open, rolling country between the Vale of York and the North Sea coast, just north of the Humber around the fine old market town of Beverley.

Beverley is 55 miles from Leeds, 95 miles from Manchester, 120 miles from Newcastle, and 135 miles from Birmingham.

The principal attraction of Beverley is the Minster, which rears above the rooftops of the town, an expanse of glowing golden stone. Beverley Minster was founded in the 8th century, but the present church was built from about 1220 and is acknowledged to be the finest Gothic church of its size in Europe. A place to put Chartres in the shade...or so the locals say.

I would hardly go that far but the exterior is magnificent and the interior warm and friendly, typical of churches which have retained an active congregation. The Minster has some wonderful stained glass and notable carvings on the stalls in the choir. The 68 misericord seats are the largest such collection in Britain, but can only be inspected accompanied by a verger.

There is the richly decorated canopy on the 14th-century Percy tomb, one of the masterpieces of medieval European art, and the tomb of the founder, St John of Beverley, who died in AD721; this grand church should certainly be the first place to visit in Beverley.

The Minster stands in the centre of the town and since parking is difficult and the town small, it makes sense to tour Beverley on foot. As a base there is the Beverley Arms Hotel in North Bar Within, a street set inside the town's remaining medieval gateway. The Beverley Arms is a hotel with a history, which always helps.

Dick Turpin, the highwayman, would rest his horse, Black Bess, here between holding up coaches on the Great North Road. Another resident was the novelist Anthony Trollope, who stayed at the hotel while seeking election as Beverley's Member of Parliament; he failed.

The present Beverley Arms dates from the latter half of the 18th century and has a Georgian facade, which fits in well with the rest of the town's architecture, for Beverley is essentially a Georgian town. The local tourist board lists 40 buildings from various architectural periods, many now serving as antique shops, art galleries or gift shops. Among them is a pub in the market square called The Push; close questioning of the bar staff failed to reveal the origin of the name, but the bar snacks are good.

The Market Cross in the main square dates from 1714, the Sun Inn from the 16th century, and Toll Gavel street goes back a further 300 years. Beverley's streets sometimes have remarkably long names like Fishmarketmoorgate, which according to the town guide means 'The street leading past the fishmarket to the moor'.

Weekend visitors can also enjoy the market held every Saturday in Saturday Market Place and, confusingly, in Wednesday Market Place. And there are many antique and curio shops in the strangely named '... And Albert', a complex of 26 small shops and boutiques near the Minster.

Another place well worth inspection is St Mary's church in North Bar, which among other curiosities contains an epitaph to two Danish soldiers, one of whom killed the other in a duel in 1689, and the carving of a white rabbit which is said to have been the inspiration for Tenniel's illustration of the White Rabbit in *Alice in Wonderland*. Beverley was a centre for the medieval Northern Gild of Minstrels, some of whose members are depicted in stone carvings in the church.

Beverley is full of such vignettes but the town's attractions are not limited to the medieval world. It also contains the Museum of Army Transport which houses a Beverley aircraft (of course), plus trucks and jeeps and amphibious craft and all manner of machines for carting men and stores about. Then there is the Guildhall, built in 1762, and the town cinema, The Picture

Gild figures - St Mary's Church, Beverley

Playhouse, which opened in 1911 and claims, with some reason, to be the oldest working cinema in the country.

Beverley can be explored with the aid of an illustrated leaflet from the TIC, or on the Ghost Walk, which begins at the Guildhall and takes in the creepier parts of the town. Exploring Beverley on one or other of these walks or on a private foray will take about a day; then it is time to drive out for a look at the Yorkshire Wolds.

The Yorkshire Wolds are shaped like a boomerang, with the lower end close to Hull. Running north, they bend east level with the city of York to reach the sea above Flamborough Head. The Wolds are not high, climbing to no more than 500ft (152m), but these slight hills offer a great number of pleasing views. This is also splendid walking country, spanned by the Wolds Way long-distance footpath, which runs from the Humber all the way north and east to Filey on the Yorkshire coast. To get a flavour of the Wolds there is a 45-mile tourist trail which begins in Beverley, heading out through the North Bar Gate.

Take the A1079 past Beverley Racecourse to the pretty village of Bishop Burton. This has black and white architecture, a duckpond and a fine pub with yet another unusual name, Altisidora, after a horse which won the St Leger in 1813. The village church is very old and another landmark here is a bust of John Wesley, founder of the Methodists, carved from the wood of the village elm under which he used to preach.

From Bishop Burton take the road to Etton and South Dalton. The church spire at Dalton Holme is no less than 200ft (61m) high and can be seen for miles. Nearby is Kiplingcotes Farm which has the distinction of hosting the country's oldest horse race, the 'Kiplingcotes Derby', held here every year since 1519. Then comes Market Weighton, another charming little town, well worth exploring before setting off for the twin villages of North Cliffe and South Cliffe, and so to Hotham.

By now it will have dawned on the visitor that the Wolds are horse country, and at North Newbald near Hotham stands the Northern Shire Horse Centre. This route leads through South Cave, where walkers can follow the Wolds Way for half an hour up to the crest of the Wolds. From South Cave the road forges on to Little Weighton and the village of Skidby.

Skidby has two attractions, the Half Moon Inn, which is famous for its Yorkshire puddings - so try to get here by lunchtime - and the Skidby windmill, the last survivor of the many mills which once crowned the tops of the Wolds. From here it is a short run back into Beverley, north across the A1079 road.

Apart from the Wolds there is the South Yorkshire coast, which lies no more than 15 miles east of Beverley and is full of pretty places. One place certainly worth stopping for on the way to the sea is Burton Agnes Hall, a magnificent example of late Elizabethan architecture, with splendid gardens containing a maze, a giant-sized chessboard (echoes of *Alice* again) and over 2,000 different varieties of plants.

The house, which is still lived in by the descendants of the original family, has beautifully carved walls in the Great Hall and an impressive picture collection in the Long Gallery, along with other treasures acquired over 400 years.

Beverley, the Wolds and the Yorkshire Coast, with the city of York less than an hour away, contain all the elements for a stimulating week-end break, at any time of the year.

INFORMATION:

BEVERLEY LIES ON THE A164 BETWEEN KINGSTON-UPON-HULL AND GREAT DRIFFIELD.

THE BEVERLEY ARMS HOTEL, BEVERLEY, TEL. 0482 869241; MANOR HOUSE, WALKINGTON, TEL. 0482 881645. TIC (BEVERLEY), TEL. 0482 867430/883898.

4

Blairgowrie and Strathmore

—

The Scottish Highlands are vast and very beautiful, perfect for car touring and worth visiting at any time of year for each season has its advantages - and disadvantages. The winters can be bleak, and summer evenings plagued by the ubiquitous Highland midge, on whose existence the Scottish Tourist Board is surprisingly reticent.

My favourite seasons tend to be spring or autumn, to enjoy the country after winter has relaxed its grip, or when the golden bracken is on the slopes and the purple heather on the hill. As for where to go, I have settled for Strathmore and Blairgowrie, a small resort town just north of Perth.

Blairgowrie is 65 miles from Edinburgh, and 85 miles from Glasgow.

If you placed your finger in the centre of a map of Scotland the nearest town would probably be Blairgowrie, but location is only part of the attraction. It is nearly 40 years since I first came for a weekend's skiing in Blairgowrie, up on the night train from London, followed by a coach from Dundee and a trek up Glenshee to the single rope tow above the Devil's Elbow. A lot has changed in that time, mostly for the better.

The Devil's Elbow, that steep climbing turn on the road to Braemar that brought winter traffic to a halt, has been ironed out; a complex lift system has replaced the rope tow, there are formidable runs like the famous 'Tiger', and Blairgowrie, which was a rather drab little place, has now become lively and as smart as new paint.

As a base for a weekend I have chosen Kinloch House Hotel by Blairgowrie, just outside the town on the road to Dunkeld. Kinloch is an old Scottish mansion, built in 1840 and set in 25 acres of wooded 'policies' and parkland, looking out across Marlee Loch to the Sidlaw

Hills. Shaggy, dark red Highland cattle graze in the fields beside the drive; the house has oak-panelled walls, the bar an impressive collection of over 130 different malt whiskies, and the award-winning restaurant serves fresh local produce. The hotel will also advise on walking, pony-trekking, shooting, fishing and sightseeing.

The temptation when visiting a beautiful area like the Highlands is to stay in the countryside and just drive about admiring the scenery. This has to be part of any weekend here, but a trip to the fair city of Perth, on the River Tay, should also be on the itinerary, especially if the weather dampens your enthusiasm for outdoor activities - which can happen up here in the Highlands.

Getting to Perth is easy down the A93, across the vale of Strathmore, and the way in leads past the palace of Scone. Scone Palace used to be an abbey containing the Stone of Scone, which was said to have been used as a pillow by Abraham when he dreamed of the stairway to Paradise. Edward I of England seized the Stone in the 14th century and it now forms part of the Coronation Chair in Westminster Abbey, though a group of Scottish nationalists took it back to Scotland for a while in the early 1950s.

Scone Palace has various collections, of furniture, clocks, needlework and ivory, while the park contains a pinetum and Moot Hill, where Scottish kings were once crowned - sitting on the Stone of Scone.

Perth stands beside the Tay, and there are good walks along the river bank, but wise visitors explore the city on foot by following the Old Perth Trail set out in a leaflet available from the TIC. Those who prefer shopping to history will find a mass of shops in the St John's Centre, which occupies a whole block between South Street and the High Street.

The High Street is lined with good shops and decorated with colourful displays of flowers. Sights to see here include the Perth Theatre and a side street with the strange name of Cutlog Vennel.

Highland bull

25

The Trail then leads into Mill Street where, appropriately, there is an old mill, now transformed into a Visitors' Centre but still selling stone-ground flour. On then through more pleasant streets and eventually to the home of Sir Walter Scott's famous character, Hal o' the Wynd, from *The Fair Maid of Perth*. The house of the Maid herself, who in real life was Catherine Glover, daughter of a local trader, still stands in North Port by the river and is now a craft shop.

The spirit of Scott hangs over Perth and there is a statue of the writer in South Inch square; but a writer even more closely associated with the city is John Buchan, author of *The Thirty-Nine Steps*, who was born in Perth in 1875 and, as Lord Tweedsmuir, became Governor-General of Canada.

Perth has a lot of history and two excellent public gardens, the Branklyn Garden, now owned by the National Trust for Scotland, and Bell's Cherrybank Gardens which will interest serious gardeners because it contains the National Heather Collection. Other places worth a stop include the Caithness Glass Factory and the Dewar's Whisky Bottling Plant, both of which have shops.

On the way back towards Blairgowrie the town of Coupar Angus has the ruins of a large Cistercian abbey, founded in 1164, and a tolbooth (gaol) which dates from 1762. Another sight en route is the imposing Meikleour Beech Hedge, which is over 100ft (30m) high and 600 yards (549m) long, and composed of trimmed beech trees. It stands on the A93 south of Blairgowrie, was planted in 1746, and is in the *Guinness Book of Records* as the highest hedge in the world. On the A9 at Bankfoot, a few miles north of Perth, is another of those motoring meccas, the Highland Motor Heritage Centre, which contains a large collection of historic and classic cars.

Blairgowrie has plenty of shops selling shortbread and tartan and is linked to the town of Rattray across the river Ericht. The Ericht is a salmon stream with an excellent walk along the banks to the spot called Donald Cargill's Leap. Another good way to explore the countryside around Blairgowrie is by mountain bike, an activity that is growing in popularity.

From Blairgowrie there are good car tours in all directions but most visitors will head over the hills to the north, past the Bridge of Cally and through Glen Shee to Deeside and Braemar. The route through Glen Shee into Deeside is the highest main road pass in Britain at 2,182ft (665m), and if the ski lifts and ski shops have done little for the landscape, the views are generally magnificent. The chief attraction along Deeside is the Royal Family's summer home and estate at Balmoral, but the whole area is beautiful and dotted with small hotels ideal for lunch or one of those tasty high teas.

West of Blairgowrie the road to Dunkeld runs beside a series of lochs, each a centre for birdwatchers and fishermen. South of Dunkeld lies Macbeth country, for here is the Birnam Wood which marched to nearby Dunsinane in Shakespeare's 'Scottish play'. Just north of Dunkeld on the A9 is the Hermitage, or Ossians Hall, built in 1758 and set in parkland, with a lovely short walk through the woods beside the River Braan.

Dunkeld is an attractive little town, with a cathedral and some well-preserved 17th-century houses along Cathedral Street. From Dunkeld it is only about 20 miles through the beautiful country of Strathbraan and over the hills past Glen Almond to the spa town of Crieff. Crieff is one of those classic Edwardian resorts, with plenty of hotels and the whisky distillery of Glenturret, one of the better known Highland Malts. The distillery can be visited, the whisky is fine, but it might be better to wait until the driving is over before sampling too much of it.

There is a lot more to see and do in and around Blairgowrie and Strathmore, but the real attraction of the Highlands is the great sense of space and the absence of crowds - outside the summer months, of course.

INFORMATION:

BLAIRGOWRIE LIES AT THE JUNCTION OF THE A93 NORTH FROM PERTH TOWARDS BRIDGE OF CALLY AND GLENSHEE, AND THE A926 BETWEEN KIRRIEMUIR AND DUNKELD.

KINLOCH HOUSE HOTEL, BLAIRGOWRIE, TEL. 025 0884 237; PARKLANDS HOTEL, PERTH, TEL. 0738 22451. TIC (BLAIRGOWRIE), TEL. 0250 872960/873701.

5

Bradford-on-Avon

—

Bradford-on-Avon is a little jewel of a town, somewhat overshadowed by the better known attractions of Bath, which is just nine miles away. Bradford, which has its own distinctive appeal and is none the worse for being less of a target for tourists, can offer all the necessary ingredients for a good weekend break.

Bradford-on-Avon is 20 miles from Bristol, 65 miles from Cardiff, 105 miles from Birmingham, and 110 miles from London.

Bradford-on-Avon was a wool town. The wool trade died out at the turn of the century but endowed Bradford with many fine buildings in the attractive local limestone. The town is a small, huddled, cosy place which looks all of a piece, set astride the River Avon. It is surprisingly hilly, and hell to park in, so the first thing to do is to get rid of the car.

Bradford-on-Avon can be easily explored on foot. It lies on a series of steep terraces but the main attractions are at river level, beginning with the wonderful Saxon church, which was built around AD700 by monks from Malmesbury Abbey. It then vanished for about a thousand years and was rediscovered in 1856.

To lose an entire church may seem an unlikely thing to do, but when the old church had been screened by other buildings and the interior converted into cottages, it was hard for anyone to see what it actually was.

The rediscovery was due to a local vicar who read about an old church of St Lawrence at Bradford in the records of Malmesbury Abbey, noticed the cruciform shape of the cottages and finally realised what he was looking at. Surrounding houses were pulled down, the interior was cleared out and the church of St Lawrence can now be seen as a pure

Saxon building, erected a full century before Alfred the Great became King of Wessex.

St Lawrence's is very small, just 38ft (11.5m) long, solidly built and rather dark; but this is a rare survivor, well worth inspection. So too are the various bridges that cross the river nearby, including the 14th-century Barton packhorse bridge, and the Town Bridge, which is graced with a small stone structure known as the chapel but which was actually the town lock-up. This can be deduced from the metal bars across the small windows. The bridge has stood here for hundreds of years; two of the arches are 13th-century and the rest date back to the 17th, the whole structure standing up remarkably well to the weight of modern traffic.

From the river the town rises up in a series of terraces supporting weavers' cottages. Newtown has the Barton Steps up from Barton Orchard, a street of picturesque dwellings behind which lies the Lady's Well. This is actually a spring which supplied the weavers with fresh water. The old Town Hall is crowned by a magnificent cupola, and from there it is a stiff climb up Conigre Hill to Middle Rank, the middle terrace, where the 17th-century cottages have long since been converted into attractive homes, their silver-coloured walls graced by roses and hollyhocks.

Above the middle terrace lies Tory, which has nothing to do with politics but takes its name from the Saxon word 'tor' meaning 'a high place'. The cottages have been well restored but the main attraction of Tory is the Chapel of St Mary Tory, which was a medieval hospice for pilgrims to the Holy Rood at Glastonbury. There are marvellous views from the garden at St Mary's, across the Vale of Wiltshire.

Back down at river level, past the old butchers' street known as The Shambles, there are two places left to see. The first is the Tithe Barn near the Kennet and Avon Canal, which runs through the town parallel to the river and is busy with narrowboats and other canal traffic, and has a popular towpath walk of a couple of miles to the Avoncliff aqueduct. The tithe barn dates from the 14th century and at 170ft (52m) long by 33ft (10m) wide is one of the largest in England.

The second place is The Hall, an Elizabethan house on the river to the east of the town, built in the early 17th century by a local cloth merchant. The gardens are very fine and contain a magnificent eight-sided dovecote. Close by is Woolley Grange, a Jacobean manor which is now a country house hotel. Here too the gardens are a picture.

A cup of tea will now be needed and can be obtained at the Bridge Teahouse, opposite the Town Bridge. The house dates from 1675 but the café is decorated with Victorian memorabilia, which extends to the uniforms worn by the waitresses.

The old 'lock-up', Bradford-on-Avon

Five miles from Bradford-on-Avon to the west is Homewood Park Hotel at Hinton Charterhouse. The hotel is set in a Georgian building with later Victorian additions, standing on the foundations of a 13th-century abbot's house and overlooking the beautiful green valley of Limpley Stoke.

The hotel has won all manner of awards including the 'Hotel of the Year' award, and is noted for its excellent restaurant. For recreation the hotel has a tennis court and croquet lawn, as well as some good walks. A half-hour stroll will take visitors to The Stag at Hinton Charterhouse, or to The Inn at Freshford, while down the valley lies the lovely Limpley Stoke, an hour away at a gentle pace. From near Limpley Stoke it is also possible to take an electrically-powered Bath & Dundas canal boat on a five-mile cruise into the city of Bath.

New visitors to the area should allow time for Bath, which rightly remains one of this country's most outstanding tourist attractions. There you can see the Pump Room, the Abbey, the Royal Crescent and of course the famous Roman Baths. Take time as well to notice the little things, like the wide alleyways that would permit the passage of sedan chairs. Bath has many fine pubs and restaurants and a number of interesting art galleries and museums, including the Museum of Costume, which has one room devoted to the history of knickers! For something different there is the American Museum at Claverton, just outside the city, which is full of American rural memorabilia culled from different parts of the United States - and has a wonderful view over the surrounding countryside.

One way to discover those sights that the mass of visitors miss is to ask local people for their recommendations. Several insisted that the gardens of The Courts at Holt, a National Trust property two miles east of Bradford-on-Avon, is a 'must' for anyone who loves gardens. The house is not open to the public but the gardens alone justify a visit. Other places hereabouts which should be seen include the much more famous gardens at Stourhead, near Warminster, and, closer to Bradford, the village of Lacock and Lacock Abbey.

Lacock today is a tiny village but 200 years ago it was a town with a thriving market. It now belongs to the National Trust, who keep it more or less as it was in the 18th century, with no televison aerials to spoil the rooftops, plenty of soft-stone cottages, a medieval tithe barn and a museum devoted to the life and work of William Henry Fox Talbot, who is credited with the invention of photography in around 1835. Lacock Abbey was founded in 1232, and became the home of the Talbots following Henry VIII's dismantling of monasteries throughout the land. Abbey and village are quite beautiful and should not be missed on any visit to Bradford-on-Avon.

INFORMATION:

BRADFORD-ON-AVON LIES ON THE A363 BETWEEN BATH AND TROWBRIDGE.

HOMEWOOD PARK HOTEL, TEL. 0225 723731; WOOLLEY GRANGE HOTEL, BRADFORD-ON-AVON, TEL. 0225 864705; THE MOAT HOUSE, PUCKLECHURCH, TEL. 0272 372283. TIC (BRADFORD-ON-AVON), TEL. 0225 865797.

6

Brecon Beacons and the Black Mountains

—

The country beyond the Wye Valley tends to be overwhelmed by the beauty of the valley itself. While the Wye Valley is certainly splendid, the Black Mountains and the Brecon Beacons National Park further west rank as some of the finest and wildest country in Britain.

These hills are ideal for outdoor activities, from walking and pony-trekking to hang-gliding and salmon fishing. Throw in a number of fine historic towns and a great many pretty villages, in a region endowed with plenty of good hotels, and a weekend in the Brecons or the Black Mountains becomes almost irresistible. From late spring to late autumm the area is perfect, but it can be wet and bleak between November and February.

Hereford, where we begin, is 55 miles from Bristol or Birmingham, 60 miles from Cardiff, and 135 miles from London.

Hereford is a very old town straddling the River Wye and noted for its cathedral, which in turn is noted for possessing the Mappa Mundi, a map of the world which was drawn in 1289. Although showing Hereford, the map leaves out the United States - an omission that was bothering a group of American visitors on the day I dropped in.

Hereford Cathedral is a splendid place with flaming glass, a 13th-century Lady Chapel, and on certain evenings of the week, a good choir. As usual the centre of the city is difficult to park in, so the best way to see Hereford is to roam about on foot.

Sights to see include the crooked spire of All Saints' church, the Old House in St Peter's Street, a black-and-white, half-timbered building dating from 1621, and the shops and cafés in and around High Town, the area near the cathedral.

The Old House has been restored and refurnished in 17th-century style, complete with four-poster beds, and cauldrons in the kitchen. The Hereford Open Air Market occupies much of High Town on Saturday and for light refreshment there is the Antique Tea Room in St Peter's Street, and some good pubs, especially the Salmon Inn in Hampton Park Road.

Hereford repays a little attention, for not only is it a fine market town, but it has also been home to some distinguished people. The Elgar Trail starts in Hereford, tracing the life of that most popular English composer, and Charles II's beguiling mistress, the kind-hearted Nell Gwynne, was born here in 1650.

The local tourist board runs a guided walk around the city, a walk which takes in all the main sights. Places to be seen include the Cider Museum, The City Museum and Art Gallery and the St John Medieval Museum at Coningsby, which features the history of the Knights of St John and the Crusades.

The Black Mountains lie to the west of Hereford and since all the roads across the mountains run north to

Brecon Beacons

south, the only way to Hay-on-Wye is to skirt the mountains to the north and follow the river, either on the B4352 or the B4349 - which runs west to the Golden Valley and then north through Vowchurch and Peterchurch to the Book Town of Britain.

That ought to be the Secondhand Book Town of Britain. Second-hand bookshops have flourished in Hay since Richard Booth opened his first shop there 20 years ago. Now it is full of them, some of considerable size like the Hay Cinema Bookshop, some more special-ised. There are books here by the shopful, but an hour spent browsing revealed few bargains. Hay also has a castle and walks along the Wye, and plenty of pubs and cafés, notably the Blue Boar in Castle Street, or the Black Lion in Lion Street.

Like Hereford, Hay has a 'High Town' area in the centre, which contains the Hay Makers Centre, a collection of artists' workshops and galleries featuring a potter, print maker, wood turner, bookbinder, silk weaver and so on. There are antique shops in Market Street, a daily market by the Market Hall selling produce from local farms, and Oscar's Bistro for a quick drink or a coffee before setting off into the nearby hills.

Hay is a good touring base, close to both the Black Mountains and the Brecon Beacons National Park. The Swan at Hay Hotel was built in 1821 and rebuilt in 1987 to provide some up-market accommodation in the area. Apart from comfortable rooms and good food, the hotel has three rods of salmon-fishing beats along the Wye, though these have to be booked in advance. The hotel can advise on other local activities including hot-air ballooning, golf, pony-trekking and canoeing, all of which are available within a few miles of The Swan.

For a short excursion there is the trip to Llanthony Priory, some miles to the south. This can be reached in various ways, most easily by car, but more adventurously on foot along the Offa's Dyke long-distance footpath. This comes through Hay and out past Hay Bluff, the escarpment which overhangs the town (a place where hang-gliders gather to launch themselves into space), then all the way along the crest to Llanthony.

This is a very good walk of about seven miles from the car park at

Hay Bluff, but boots are essential and some rain gear advisable. Care is needed in coming down to the priory on the valley floor. Llanthony is very picturesque and photogenic, and lunches are available at the priory or at the nearby pub. Do not leave the Llanthony Valley without going south to see the church of St Martin at Cwmyoy, which is so warped and twisted by subsidence that there is hardly a straight line or wall in the entire place.

A whole weekend could be taken up exploring the moors and valleys around Hereford and Hay, but there is more to see further to the west. Take the B4350 out of Hay past the hamlet of Three Cocks, where the Three Cocks Hotel is another good place to stay or visit for lunch, then on to the town of Brecon.

The Brecon Beacon National Park, covering more than 500 square miles, is a splendid region of hills and open ridges, especially around the peak of Pen y Fan which rises to 2,907ft (886m) along the spine of the Beacons south of Brecon. On a brief visit the traveller will find enough walking to do around the town of Brecon and in the hills around Pen y Fan.

The best place to begin is at the Brecon Beacons Mountain Centre near Libanus, five miles south of Brecon on the road to Pen y Fan. The centre is full of information and advice on what to see and where to go, together with tips regarding routes and the ever-changeable local weather.

There are plenty of other distractions with sailing, windsurfing and canoeing on the lake at Llangorse. Another enjoyable excursion would be a cruise on the Monmouth and Brecon Canal, a two-and-a-half-hour trip above the River Usk.

While the main appeal of the Black Mountains and the Brecons is the opportunity for outdoor activities, this is also an excellent area for touring with plenty of attractions in the shape of gardens, castles, small villages and viewpoints to add variety to a day in the car. If you want to go walking - and not to go walking here would be a shame - then comfortable boots are essential. All the Tourist Information Centres and most of the hotels are full of advice on good local walks of every distance and degree of difficulty, and there are waymarked trails from every town and village. As a backdrop to all this there is some spectacular mountain scenery and, outside one or two main centres, not too many people.

INFORMATION:

HEREFORD LIES AT THE JUNCTION OF THE A49 FROM LEOMINSTER TO ROSS-ON-WYE WITH THE A438 FROM LEDBURY TO HAY-ON-WYE.

THE SWAN AT HAY HOTEL, HAY-ON-WYE, TEL. 0497 821188; THREE COCKS HOTEL, THREE COCKS, NEAR BRECON, TEL. 0497 847215. TIC (BRECON), TEL. 0874 622485; TIC (HEREFORD), TEL. 0432 268430.

7

Buxton and the Dark Peak

—

The Peak District is one of the most beautiful parts of England, a rolling upland plateau, seamed with steep-sided river valleys, picked out with drystone walls and well supplied with pretty villages. It is an excellent place for a weekend break, anytime outside the depths of winter when the area can become alarmingly bleak. Otherwise there are good walks, historic houses, spa towns, unusual folkloric events and a compact countryside, quite easy to explore.

Buxton is 60 miles from Leeds, 70 miles from Birmingham, 150 miles from Newcastle, and 165 miles from London.

The Peak District is described by the local tourist board as 'England's most accessible Highlands', which, with due acknowledgement to Scotland, is fair comment, for the Peak District is definitely hilly.

Buxton lies in the heart of the Peak, the ideal centre for touring the entire area, but especially the parts to the north. Most of the region is contained within the Peak District National Park, which covers an area of some 540 square miles and includes parts of Staffordshire, Cheshire, Yorkshire and Derbyshire.

The Peak District is roughly divided into two areas, the 'Dark Peak' in the north, where the rock is millstone grit, and the 'White Peak' in the south, where the paler limestone prevails. These rocks colour the houses and the walls, dark in the north, lighter in the south, and come together in the town of Bakewell, where half the houses seem to be of millstone and the rest of limestone. The northern part contains the higher hills like Kinder Scout which, at 2,088ft (636m), is the highest point in the Dark Peak area, also known as the 'High Peak'.

Three Shires Head

The Palace Hotel in Buxton is a good base for a weekend, a Victorian hotel, built in 1868, which has catered for the 'carriage trade' ever since. Like a lot of Victorian hotels the Palace is quite imposing, which is not surprising since the architect was Henry Curry, who worked for the Duke of Devonshire at Chatsworth. The grandeur still remains but the hotel now has a Leisure Centre, complete with sauna and solarium, lots of comfortable public rooms and good food in the Dovedale Restaurant.

The other grand hotel hereabouts is even older. The Old Hall in Buxton was built by the Earl of Shrewsbury in the 16th century, and one of the first guests was Mary, Queen of Scots, who arrived here under guard in 1573. She enjoyed the warm spa waters, which have attracted visitors to Buxton since Roman times. The waters can still be sampled at St Anne's Well, where they bubble up at a tongue-testing 82°F (28°C).

Apart from the area around the Crescent, where there are parks and gardens, Buxton is a no-nonsense kind of place and not over decorative. There is a good range of shops and, for entertainment, Buxton Opera

House, the centrepiece of the annual Buxton Festival, which puts on everything from Gilbert and Sullivan to panto and variety shows.

Other local attractions include the stalagmite and stalactite-infested Poole's Cavern, described as 'The Wonder of the Peak' by the writer Charles Cotton as long ago as 1680. The cave is lit by arc lights which pick out the vivid colours in the stone. When you finally surface you can wander around the 100 acres of woodland that comprise Buxton Country Park.

The main reason for visiting the Peak District is the countryside, so the first thing to acquire in Buxton is a walking guide. The Peak abounds with good walks and every hotel, bookshop and TIC is awash with maps and guides. Peak District walking is the real thing, requiring good boots, walking shoes or stout trainers, plus a wind- or rainproof jacket in a small rucksack.

The Dark Peak is also ideal for car touring, on quiet but narrow roads which lead to idyllic places. To give one example, take the A6, north from Buxton to Chapel-en-le-Frith, a pleasant market town, dating back to the 13th century. At Chapel-en-le-Frith turn east and follow minor roads for the village of Castleton.

Castleton is a centre for walkers, cavers and lovers of geology. It lies at the bottom of the Winnats Pass, below the crest of Mam Tor, which is easily identified since it is always circled by hang-gliders.

The hills around Castleton are riddled with mines and caverns producing the famous Blue John stone. Blue John was discovered during lead mining and the polished stone is now sold for necklaces, lamp-stands, vases and ashtrays. This semi-precious stone is found only in Castleton, and there is an impressive display of Blue John artifacts in the Ollerenshaw Collection at Cavendish House there.

The show caves like the Treak Cliff Cavern or the Speedwell Cavern, which offers a boat ride on an underground river, attract a great many visitors. Others gather at Peveril Castle above the village, or take a walk up to a nearby ridge to enjoy the views.

A mile or so north of Castleton lies Edale, a walkers' mecca and the start of the Pennine Way. Rugged, well-equipped backpackers can be seen starting out on this classic trek; but for something less demanding there is the half-day walk from Edale up to the summit of Kinder Scout, via Jacob's Ladder, a fine walk with red grouse whirring away from under your boots. Other birds here include the golden plover and the curlew.

It is possible to spend a full day around Castleton, but there are plenty of other attractions. The Ladybower Reservoir, north-east of Castleton, was used as a practice run by the 'Dambusters' squadron before the raid on Germany's dams in May 1943, and is now a centre for watersports. Many of the village shops hire out mountain bikes for trips across the moors or for tours around Ladybower Reservoir.

Following the A625 east from Castleton will bring the traveller to Hathersage and the Hathersage Inn, a very friendly pub and small hotel where the Cricketer's Bar serves good pub snacks and is decorated not only with bails, stumps and pads, but on summer Saturdays, with the local cricket team.

Hathersage is also famous locally as the birthplace of Little John, the companion of Robin Hood, and there is a Little John pub on the main street. Climbers come to Hathersage to attempt the gritstone ridges on Stanage Edge close by.

The country south of Hathersage contains the village of Eyam, the setting for a very gallant tale. During the Great Plague of 1665 a tailor in Eyam received a parcel of clothes from London, and with it the plague germ. Within days, the villagers were infected, but they came to a terrible decision. Rather than flee and save themselves at the risk of spreading the infection to surrounding places, they would quarantine themselves within the village and wait it out.

Over the next few months most of the Eyam villagers died. They were buried where they fell, and the gravestones can be seen in the churchyard and around the village, a memorial to a very unusual piece of self-sacrifice. Eyam today is a quiet and pretty place with good views over the Peak from the surrounding ridges.

This is the way to see the Dark Peak, wandering on foot or by car from place to place. From Eyam it is no distance to Bakewell, home of the Bakewell tart, and the place which marks the divide between the

White and Dark Peak. The history of the Peak National Park is displayed in the Exhibition Centre in the Market Hall; there are good walks along the River Wye, and it is no distance to historic houses like Chatsworth and Haddon Hall just to the south.

Although the places featured in this account are in the Dark Peak, north and east of Buxton, there is no need for any visitor to be so restricted. There is still the moorlands around the Cat and Fiddle Pass and Wildboarclough to the west, and good walks along the Windgather Rocks and in the Macclesfield Forest. Once you start exploring the Peak District, you are sure to want to come again.

INFORMATION:

BUXTON LIES ON THE A6 BETWEEN BAKEWELL AND CHAPEL-EN-LE-FRITH.

THE PALACE HOTEL, BUXTON, TEL. 0298 22001; THE OLD HALL, BUXTON, TEL. 0298 22841; THE HATHERSAGE INN, HATHERSAGE, TEL. 0433 650259. TIC (BUXTON), TEL. 0298 25106.

8

Carmarthen and Tenby

—

After William the Conqueror invaded England in 1066 and won the Battle of Hastings, some of his knights sailed off to make a landing on the western coast of Wales. Over the next few decades the Normans established their rule and set up the Earldom of Pembroke, far beyond the Anglo-Welsh frontier. There they remained until Edward I conquered the Principality in the 13th century and linked Pembroke to the rest of his kingdom.

This is the origin of Pembrokeshire, the 'little England beyond Wales', now part of Dyfyd and one of the most beautiful parts of the Principality. As a base for exploring the area there is the choice of two attractive towns, Carmarthen on the River Towy, or the coastal resort of Tenby. Both are all-season destinations.

Carmarthen is 70 miles from Cardiff, and 110 miles from Bristol.

Tenby is 95 miles from Cardiff, and 135 miles from Bristol.

Carmarthen was once a Roman port. The Romans built a fine amphitheatre which was excavated in 1968 and is now one of the town's great attractions. Those who are less interested in ancient times will enjoy the small pubs, narrow streets and alleyways that lace this attractive market town. Those who like the old Celtic legends will want to know that this is the birthplace of Merlin, King Arthur's personal wizard, and in Welsh Carmarthen means 'Merlin's Town'.

The town has a large and lively market on Saturday, a golf driving range, an all-weather leisure centre, and a notably well-informed Tourist Information Centre. For something local, truly Welsh, and quite unique, there is coracle fishing on the River Towy. These round tarred boats, made of waterproofed hide stretched over a willow wood frame, feel decidedly tippy, but a coracle trip should not be missed. The TIC has full details.

Carmarthen is a first-class touring centre for West Wales and as a base for these excursions there is the Ivy Bush Royal Hotel in the town centre, a historic inn with a good bar and restaurant.

Every weekend ought to include fresh air and exercise, so a walk on the hills and moors is alway advisable. The TIC is full of suggestions for walks long and short, but just 15 miles north of Carmarthen lie the Llanllwni and Llanybyther mountains, which provide some of the finest walking in Wales. These walks fan out from the towns and villages of the Teifi Valley, places like Llanybydder, or from the main centre hereabouts, the market town of Newcastle Emlyn.

The 'new' castle here was actually built in 1240 and is one of the places that Cromwell knocked about a bit, but the grounds are beautiful, perfect for a picnic if the day is fine. There is coracle fishing from the Centre at Cenarth Falls, and birdwatchers should bring their field glasses and look out for the red kite and the buzzard. Another good excursion is a trip on the Teifi Valley Railway from the Station Yard at Llandysul, a wonderful journey in spring when the little train runs through woods carpeted with bluebells, or in summer when the banks of the cuttings are draped with willow herb and marshmallow.

Those who go south from Carmarthen will soon come to Carmarthen Bay, where they can walk on the Pembrokeshire Coastal Path, which runs through the Pembrokeshire Coast National Park. This is the part of Wales immortalised by Dylan Thomas, and the place where he lived and worked for many years, the Boat House at Laugharne, south of St Clears on the A40, has become a place of pilgrimage for lovers of his poetry.

This is where Dylan Thomas wrote *Under Milk Wood*, and the cliffside house, which is now a Heritage Centre dedicated to his life and work, offers delightful views over the Taf estuary. Dylan Thomas is buried in the churchyard of St Martin's in Laugharne.

Other places worth a look are the little fishing port and yachting centre of Ferryside, with plenty of waymarked walks, and across the water, the photogenic ruins of Llansteffan Castle and the village of

Llansteffan, another pretty spot with two good pubs serving lunches.

One of the other great sights around here is the vast sweep of Pendine Sands. This eight-mile stretch of firm, level sand, was the place where drivers came between the wars to make attempts on the Land Speed Record. Sir Malcolm Campbell captured and recaptured the record here on several occasions, but the attempts stopped in 1927 when the Welsh racing driver, Parry Thomas, crashed and died on the Sands. On a fine day Pendine Sands would not look out of place in the South Pacific, with the blue sea crashing in across the golden strand.

With only a weekend to spare the visitor must get on, and the next place to visit, or stay in, should be the resort town of Tenby. Tenby is a walled town, surrounded by high ramparts, which, say the locals, were built to keep the Welsh out.

Few small towns in Britain have so much to offer as pretty Tenby, and while I fear to weary the traveller with churches, St Mary's in the centre of the town must not be missed. Not only is it very attractive, it is full of fascinating

Dylan Thomas's 'Writing Shed'

memorials to former residents of the town. There is one to Colonel James Sleeman of the 73rd Regiment, who was born in Tenby in 1807 and died there in 1889. Colonel Sleemen spent most of his life in India where he devoted his time to stamping out the Thugs, those ritual murderers who preyed on travellers and provided the background for a famous novel by John Masters.

Then there is one to Robert Recorde, the 16th-century mathematician whose gift to the world of science was the symbol of equality, ie =, a small thing but we would be lost without it. Another memorial is to one of the town's 'bathing ladies' who ran the bathing machines on the beach from which the bathers would be seized and plunged into the foam. This lady 'died in the sea of apoplexy in her 82nd year'. St Mary's is full of such plaques and memorials.

Tenby also has a castle, fringed with antique cannon, which contains a museum covering not only the history of the town but also the work of two favourite artists, Gwen and Augustus John. The views from up on the headland there are equally eye-catching, and after that there is the walk down to the harbour for the boat ride to Caldey Island.

Before the trip to Caldey there are more delights to sample in Tenby. The Tudor Merchant's House is a fine late-medieval building well worth inspection, and the tiny fishermen's church of St Julian down by the harbour is a little gem. Another, somewhat larger gem, is the Pembrokeshire Coast National Park which lies on either side of Tenby and embraces an area of some 170 square miles of coast and countryside.

The great excursion from Tenby is the 20-minute boat ride out to Caldey Island, a marvellous way to view the rugged coast of Pembrokeshire. Caldey Island has been home to a religious community for at least 1,000 years, surviving or enduring attacks by the Vikings and the Irish pirates and all manner of other excitements. It now supports a small community of Trappist monks, who run a farm and a perfumery, manufacturing the perfume from wild flowers and herbs, and this plus a tourist shop and guesthouse for retreats keeps the community alive.

Back on the mainland there is still more to see. A little west of Tenby lies Manorbier Castle, a remarkably intact 12th-century fortress set above the beach; while some way beyond that lies St Brides Bay, another great sweep of beach that leads to the northern part of the Pembroke coast and the little city of St David's. As cities go, St David's is rather small, little more than a village, but below the village lies the great red-stone cathedral which contains the shrine of the patron saint of Wales. Close by are the remains of the 14th-century Bishop's Palace, unoccupied for the past 300 years, but no less impressive for that.

This is just a sample of all there is to see in the Little England beyond Wales. But go there soon, before the Welsh find out about it.

INFORMATION:
CARMARTHEN LIES AT THE JUNCTION OF THE A40 FROM LLANDEILO TO ST CLEARS WITH THE A485/A484 FROM LAMPETER TO KIDWELLY.

TENBY IS ON THE SOUTH COAST AT THE JUNCTION OF THE A4139 EAST FROM PEMBROKE AND THE A478 SOUTH FROM NARBERTH.

THE IVY BUSH ROYAL HOTEL, CARMARTHEN, TEL. 0267 235111; WATERWYNCH HOUSE HOTEL, TENBY, TEL. 0834 842464. TIC (CARMARTHEN), TEL. 0267 231557; TIC (TENBY), TEL. 0834 842402.

9

Chagford and Dartmoor

—

Dartmoor is best known for being wild and bleak and full of Baskervilles. It is also one of the most beautiful places in Britain in the springtime, or the early days of autumn. Spring is when the bluebells and snowdrops carpet the sheltered corners of the woods, and in September and October the gorse and heather are blazing on the hillsides below the rocky tors.

Chagford, the base for this Dartmoor weekend, is 105 miles from Britol, and 140 miles from Cardiff.

Much of Dartmoor is now protected by the Dartmoor National Park which covers an area of 365 square miles, a region of heathland and bog, deep valleys and tinkling streams, rising to 2,085ft (635m) and subject to sudden variations in the weather. On a good day Dartmoor is a paradise, but within minutes the weather can change, the clouds rush in and the heavens open. The rainfall is heavy - over 90in (229cm) a year - and in the wintertime the wind across Dartmoor can cut like a knife.

Yet, with all that, Dartmoor is wonderful. It has wild and wide open spaces and spectacular scenery, beautiful river valleys and quaint villages. Above all, Dartmoor is dramatic.

The distinctive features of Dartmoor are the tors, rocky granite outcrops from the bogs and heather which give such character to the landscape. Prehistoric man lived on Dartmoor, leaving behind relics of his passing in the shape of standing stones and stone circles. The modern occupants of Dartmoor, the farmers and smallholders, even the soldiers who come to wage war games on the ranges, have to be almost as hardy, for the moor is a demanding place.

Dartmoor can be explored by car, on foot or by bicycle or pony. The roads are narrow and sometimes cut so deeply into the valley sides and slopes that they seem like roofless tunnels. On foot across the moor it is as well to follow one of the many waymarked trails - and there are more than 500 miles of footpath on offer - or take one of the guided walks offered by the Visitors' Centres. The centres can also advise on the hire of mountain bikes or sturdy Dartmoor ponies.

Dartmoor cannot be adequately explored in a couple of days, so this weekend is restricted to the eastern edge of the moor, with the River Exe and city of Exeter further

Bowerman's Nose, Dartmoor

to the east. If the weather is bad, Exeter is the obvious place to go, with good shopping, a magnificent cathedral and a maritime museum.

Chagford has always been regarded as a good starting off point for the moor. In the 1930s one visitor wrote: 'The happiest village in England is Chagford...the people there never stop smiling and no wonder, for it lies open to the sun, on the threshold of the purple Moor, and at its feet lie the brown waters of the Teign, the loveliest of Devon rivers.' The present-day visitor would see no reason to change any of that.

Chagford is one of the four stannary towns, where the local tin miners brought their tin for weighing and sale. It is very picturesque, full of narrow streets and old houses, among which is the Three Crowns Hotel, set in a 13th-century stone building and full of legends. Various ghosts stalk the corridors of the Three Crowns, including that of a young Cavalier, Sidney Godolphin, the poet, who was wounded by musket fire at Chagford in February 1643 and died in the hotel. The hotel has old furniture and friendly people, and hosts musical evenings in the Chimney Bar where local musicians come in to entertain.

Another good hotel hereabouts is the Mill End on the banks of the River Teign. The Mill End is a Logis hotel, with good food, comfortable bedrooms and beautiful gardens running down to the river. The old mill wheel is still in place and still turning, and lessons in fly fishing can be booked with the gillie.

Close to the Mill End is Castle Drogo, one of the more unusual places in this part of Devon. Castle Drogo may look medieval but it is not very old, being built between 1910 and 1930 by Sir Edwin Lutyens, with the aim of combining medieval grandeur with 20th-century comfort.

This was just before rising costs and social change made servants an anachronism, so the castle is a relic of the more gracious if less egalitarian age between the Wars. The kitchen and dining room are splendid and the Gun Room contains an exhibit detailing the story surrounding the building of the castle.

Since Lutyens was very fond of gardens and often collaborated with Gertrude Jekyll, the grounds of Castle Drogo are especially attractive. There is a formal terrace garden with rose beds and a herbaceous border, a large croquet lawn - where visitors are invited to play - and fine walks from the garden along the ridge above the Teign and down to the banks of the river.

It is quite possible to spend an entire weekend around Chagford, visiting places like Castle Drogo and Buckland Abbey near Yelverton which was once the home of that Devon pirate, Sir Francis Drake, or towns like Crediton, Okehampton and Tiverton around the lip of the moor; but if the weather is even halfway reasonable, and it usually is for a few hours at least, the moor itself cannot be missed.

The best way to see a lot of Dartmoor in a short time is to take the B3212 road across the moor from Moretonhampstead to Princetown, past Postbridge and Two Bridges. This is a wonderful up-and-down road, running across rivers like the Bovey and the East and West Dart. Tors, like Bellever (perched above the forest of the same name) and Beardown, overlook the dramatically wild landscape.

Postbridge has a medieval clapper bridge consisting of nine huge granite slabs across the river. Local walks include a tramp for an hour or so along the Lich Way track or 'Road of the Dead', down which bodies were taken for burial at Lydford.

A little past Two Bridges lies Princetown, best known for Dartmoor Prison. The prison was built about 1806 at the height of the Napoleonic Wars to house French prisoners, who were forced to erect the building themselves in conditions of severe hardship. The prison is a grim pile even on a sunny day. Rather more attractive is the National Park Headquarters, which has a great range of books and information on Dartmoor.

Thus equipped, the sensible visitor will wander. Dartmeet, east of Two Bridges, is another beauty spot on the lateral road across the moor, the B3357, and the place where the East and West Dart finally come together. The tors above here are particularly impressive and lie in plain sight of the rolling road that runs across the high moor to Ashburton. The Friday market in Tavistock is well worth a visit. Like Chagford and Ashburton, Tavistock was a stannary town, once surrounded by tin mines.

Before ending this weekend do visit Widecombe-in-the-Moor near Dartmeet. This tiny village, the subject of one of England's best known folk songs, 'Widdicombe Fair', is a lovely little place with a great church and a good inn, where 'Old Uncle Tom Cobbleigh and all' were very happy to stop for a pint. An example we all might follow.

INFORMATION:
CHAGFORD LIES ON THE EASTERN EDGE OF DARTMOOR, JUST WEST OF EASTON, ON THE A382 RUNNING NORTH FROM MORETONHAMPSTEAD TO WHIDDON DOWN ON THE A30.

THE THREE CROWNS HOTEL, CHAGFORD, TEL. 0647 433444; MILL END HOTEL, CHAGFORD, TEL. 0647 432282. TIC (EXETER), TEL. 0392 265700; TIC (TAVISTOCK), TEL. 0822 612938.

10

Chipping Campden and the Cotswolds

—

The Cotswolds have always been a popular area for weekend breaks. The region has an abundance of man-made and natural attractions and plenty of places to stay, but my own choice as a touring centre is the market town of Chipping Campden. The Cotswolds can be bleak in winter, but no part of England is more beautiful in the other seasons of the year.

Chipping Campden is 40 miles from Birmingham, 65 miles from Bristol, 90 miles from London, and 100 miles from Cardiff.

To call this part of England the Cotswold *Hills*, as many people do, is incorrect. Although there are hills in the Cotswolds, and very steep hills at that, this is actually a high plateau, cut about by river valleys. Nor should the visitor be lulled by the present pastoral setting into assuming that the Cotswolds were ever thus, a dreamy backwater set between the bustle of London and the throbbing factories of the Midlands. Quite the contrary. During the Middle Ages this was the powerhouse of the English economy, producing the wealth of the nation, the source of which can still be seen on the Cotswold slopes - sheep.

This was one of the wealthy areas of England for most of the Middle Ages. The local wool merchants used some of the profits made from selling English wool to Flemish weavers to furnish their villages and towns with distinguished buildings and magnificent churches. Indeed, the 'wool churches' of the Cotswolds are one of the glories of England.

First though, Chipping Campden. 'Chipping' is an Old English word for market, and the town, once a centre for the wool trade, is still a centre for the local farmers. Chipping Campden has a wool church, St James's, at the top of the town, which was endowed in the early 15th century by

William Grevel - 'Flower of the Wool Merchants of all England', according to his brass in the chancel.

G.M.Trevelyan, the historian, said that Chipping Campden had 'the most beautiful high street in the whole of England', and few would disagree with that even today. This long and winding main street is lined with grey-stone houses, dating from the 17th century or earlier, with the open Market Hall as one distinctive feature.

Thanks to that original prosperity, and to a later influx of artists at the turn of the century, the centre of Chipping Campden has been spared the worst excesses of post-war development. The main street has bookshops, both new and secondhand, boutiques, pubs, cafés and craft shops, and is the perfect place to spend a Saturday morning. Two good pubs among many are The Volunteer at the bottom of the town near the Cotswold Way, and the Eight Bells in Church Street, which does a good lunch. The stonemasons stayed here while building the church,

Market Hall, Chipping Campden

and this is where the bells were kept before being hung in the tower.

As a base for a visit to Chipping Campden and the North Cotswolds there is the Charingworth Manor Hotel, two miles east of the town on the B4035. A first-class country house hotel, Charingworth has evolved from a medieval manor, and is built in that beautiful local stone.

Charingworth has a modern wing and a pool and leisure spa, but the heart of the hotel is Edward Burnel's medieval manor. The beams in the sitting room are worth inspection for they are painted with the Burnel chevrons and date from about 1316. The dining room is named in memory of John Grevile, an ancestor of that church-building wool merchant, and the bedrooms in the main building contain more beams and some four-poster beds. Beyond the spacious gardens lies a 50-acre estate.

The Cotswolds provide excellent walking country, well supplied with waymarked footpaths. There is a good half-hour walk from Charing worth Manor to the village of Ebrington, and four more of varying length detailed in *A Personal Guide to the Cotswolds*, a useful booklet written by Jane Henty, wife of the manager. Two long-distance footpaths run across the hills, the Cotswold Way which begins in Chipping Campden and runs south to Bath, and the Oxfordshire Way which meanders across the county and can be followed through the Cotswolds from village to village.

Those who want to sample just a little walking should follow the Cotswold Way out of Chipping Campden at the lower end of the high street for a couple of miles up to the breezy heights of Dover's Hill, a spot which offers splendid views over the Cotswold escarpment and the Vale of Evesham to the west.

Those who are not all that keen on walking will find a great deal to see within easy driving distance of Chipping Campden. Three miles north of the town lies the National Trust's Hidcote Manor, best known for that fragrant flower, Hidcote lavender. If that were all it had to offer, Hidcote would still be worth a visit, but the place is a gardeners' mecca. In the space of 10 acres Major Lawrence Johnston, the renowned horticulturist, created a great variety of gardens, each separated by hedges of yew or holly. There is a water garden, a herb garden, a white garden, and many more, plus spacious lawns and wonderful rose beds.

Not far away is yet another garden, equally beautiful if rather less well known, at Kiftsgate Court, a place noted for roses. After a look at that it is time to pick up the B4632 at Mickleton, on the edge of the Cotswold escarpment, and head south through the village of Weston Subedge towards Broadway.

Broadway has been described as the 'Show Village of England' and it is certainly very pretty, with the famous Lygon Arms Hotel as the focal point. Everyone who was anyone has stayed at the Lygon Arms down the centuries, including Charles I, whose bedroom, filled with contemporary furniture, is still a feature of the hotel, playing counterpoint to the modern pool and spa. A meal in the Great Hall at the Lygon Arms is a memorable experience. Broadway is inundated with trippers and tourists throughout the year, and although parking in the main street can be difficult, there is a well-signposted public car park.

For a pleasant excursion away from the bustle of Broadway, drive east along the A44 to Fish Hill, where the Fish Inn is a good country pub, and take the short walk from there, along the track of the Cotswold Way, to Broadway Tower. This 65ft-high (20m) tower, which offers marvellous views over 12 counties from the top, is open from April to October. It was built in the 1790s by the sixth Earl of Coventry as a birthday present for his wife.

After Broadway it pays to wander. This is easy as the Cotswold lanes are well signposted and it is hard to get lost. Places that should be seen include Snowshill, which has a Tudor manor house with a late 17th-century facade, now owned by the National Trust and containing a most eclectic collection gathered together by the former owner, Charles Wade. This includes Japanese armour, old bicycles, antique clocks and musical instruments. The village of Stanton is quite exquisite, and Stanway, with its manor house, is a vision in golden stone.

No stay in the Cotswolds is really complete without a visit to the 'Slaughters' and the 'Swells', four very pretty villages set on tinkling streams - with another very attractive hotel at Upper Slaughter, the Lords of the Manor. Other places which ought to be seen include the sizeable village of Northleach, which has one of the finest of all the wool churches, and Winchcombe, where there is the medieval George inn, one of the most notable pubs in the Cotswolds. Drivers will not need to be reminded that most of these pubs serve coffee, teas and lunches as well as alcoholic drinks.

If the weather is poor, Bourton-on-the-Water and the picturesque town of Burford are well supplied with tea rooms, and have antique shops and secondhand bookshops made for browsing round until the sun comes out again. North of Burford on the A436 lies a very special place, the village of Adlestrop, which gave its name to the best-remembered poem of the Great War poet, Edward Thomas. The station where his train drew in has long since been pulled down, but the station sign can still be seen, erected in a bus shelter on the outskirts of the village, with his poem reproduced on a brass plaque below.

As for evening entertainment, there are village pubs and fine country restaurants, and at Stratford-on-Avon a choice of three theatres. Personally, after a long day touring the Cotswolds, I am usually more than ready for a good dinner, and an early night.

INFORMATION:

·*CHIPPING CAMPDEN LIES ON THE B4035 BETWEEN EVESHAM AND SHIPSTON-ON-STOUR, JUST EAST OF THE B4632 FROM STRATFORD-UPON-AVON TO BROADWAY.*

CHARINGWORTH MANOR, NEAR CHIPPING CAMPDEN, TEL. 0386 78555; LORDS OF THE MANOR HOTEL, UPPER SLAUGHTER, TEL. 0451 820243; THE LYGON ARMS, BROADWAY, TEL. 0386 852255. TIC (CHIPPING CAMPDEN), TEL. 0386 840101; TIC (STOW-ON-THE-WOLD), TEL. 0451 831082.

11

Church Stretton and the Long Mynd

—

The little town of Church Stretton in Shropshire fits snugly against the eastern slopes of the Long Mynd mountain, about 12 miles south of Shrewsbury. This is great walking country, for you can get up high quickly and the sharp rise of the hills from the Cheshire Plains gives extensive views and a great feeling of space, out of proportion to the actual height of the hills.

This part of Britain offers great scope for outdoor activities, with some historic towns to amuse those people who are less interested in shinning up the nearby heights. It is a place for all seasons with plenty to do at every time of year.

Church Stretton is 50 miles from Birmingham, 100 miles from Cardiff, and 115 miles from Bristol.

In late Victorian times the burghers of Church Stretton decided to turn the town into a spa, an inventive enterprise as there are no springs nearby. For a while they brought the waters in by train from Llandrindod Wells, but while you cannot actually 'take the waters' here, the Victorians knew a good spot for a weekend break and a visit to Church Stretton combines a good deal of sightseeing with some activity in the local hills.

Had the Victorians got their spa established it would have been in the building that now houses the Longmynd Hotel. This stands high above the town and offers a wide variety of facilities, with great views over Caer Caradoc hill and the sharp ridge of Wenlock Edge.

There is also the Mynd House Hotel at Little Stretton. This unpretentious building was erected in Edwardian times by a Wolverhampton businessman who travelled every Friday to his country residence and kept a staff of six. The present owners, recognising there was not much they could do about the outside of the building, have concentrated on providing attractive suites, gourmet food and a wine list that was declared the 'Best in Britain' in 1991, with over 250 wines, a large number available in half-bottles.

The Mynd House has its own guide detailing short walks from the hotel. One of these leads to the Acton Scott Historic Working Farm, which evokes the history of the Shropshire farming community of a century ago. You can see shire horses and rare breeds of farm animals, and the farrier, blacksmith and wheelwright at work.

Church Stretton has a TIC at the library, where visitors can pick up a Town Trail leaflet to guide them through the major sights and features. There is also a good range of maps and guides suggesting walks or drives in the area, to the Long Mynd and the lonelier Stiperstones beyond.

The slopes of the Long Mynd can be reached by car, taking the road west from the town centre, the Burway. The road rises steeply and you are soon high up in an Area of Outstanding Natural Beauty, 5,000 acres of upland moor owned by the National Trust.

If you prefer to walk in a more sheltered area, try Carding Mill Valley, which is signposted from the town centre. There are plenty of car parks here, near the National Trust café and shop, with easy walks to the New Pool Reservoir or the Lightspout Waterfall.

The Stiperstones is a series of rocky outcrops lying to the west of the Long Mynd, along a ridge above an old lead-mining area. The highest of these outcrops is known as the 'Devil's Chair', and it is said that when low cloud or mist cloaks the tops of the Stiperstones, the Devil is sitting in his chair.

To the east lies Wenlock Edge, more good walking country. The roads on either side of the Edge lead to the Ironbridge Gorge, one of Britain's World Heritage sites, the birthplace of the Industrial Revolution 250 years ago. Here they made the first iron rails and wheels to run on them, iron bridges and boats to sail under them, and steam locomotives to go over them. Note the construction of the bridge because the builders used carpentry techniques to put it together. Coalport china was developed with Coalbrookdale castings, and this heritage is preserved in seven main museums and a variety of smaller sites, open seven days a week and absolutely fascinating.

In the opposite direction, past the Green Dragon Inn in Little Stretton and through Craven Arms - a place not a pub - you will travel further back in time. Turn right to Stokesay and visit the castle, one of the most perfectly preserved examples of an early fortified manor house in England. It was built 700 years ago by Laurence of Ludlow, a wealthy wool merchant, and has remained virtually unaltered. It is delightfully situated and a good place for a picnic, with the castle and church and gatehouse in the foreground and the Shropshire hills as the backdrop.

From Stokesay, Ludlow is just 10 minutes away down the A49 and worth a long and leisurely stop. The town is beautiful and reflects much that is worthy in British vernacular architecture. There are over 500 listed buildings in the town, ranging from 14th-century timber-frame houses to elegant Georgian mansions. It all fits together in a homogeneous and delightful way and the Norman castle crowns the lot.

To get the feel of how the castle dominates the town, drive or walk down to Dinham Bridge and the Linney Riverside Park and take a rowing boat out on the Teme. You can row up river for half a mile or so and the castle towers above in a most dramatic fashion. This trip deserves a cream tea afterwards on the terrace of the Dinham Weir Hotel, which sits on the site of an old mill, close to the bridge.

A visit to the castle or a walk round its moat should follow, and then an exploration of the town. The TIC has a good booklet, *Ludlow Walks*, which take in all the buildings of note.

That done, tired sightseers in need of refreshment should make for De Grey's Café, which dates from 1570. For a pub lunch, try the Church Inn on the corner of King Street and Church Street.

Then there is The Feathers in the Bull Ring, though the prize for the oldest inn in Ludlow goes to The Bull just across the road. The Feathers is definitely the most handsome inn hereabouts and its extraordinary timber frontage hides a watering hole of elegance and distinction.

Ludlow is a national treasure and it is worthwhile leaving the town by the old packhorse bridge over the Teme, which takes you south into the

Stokesay Castle

hamlet of Ludford. Immediately over the bridge, turn right and this will bring you onto the heights of Whitcliffe, ancient common land that has a superb view of the castle and the town; and another good picnic spot.

Continue through Bringewood Chase and you will reach Leintwardine and can circle northwards through the delightfully named Clungunford, and so back to Little Stretton.

INFORMATION:

CHURCH STRETTON LIES ON THE A49 BETWEEN LUDLOW AND SHREWSBURY.

MYND HOUSE HOTEL, LITTLE STRETTON, TEL. 0694 722212; DINHAM WEIR HOTEL, DINHAM BRIDGE, TEL. 0584 874431; THE FEATHERS, LUDLOW, TEL. 0584 875261. TIC (CHURCH STRETTON), TEL. 0694 723133; TIC (LUDLOW), TEL. 0584 875053.

12

Cranbrook and the Weald of Kent

—

The Weald of Kent is archetypal England, with the additional lure of hop fields and oast houses, sandwiched between the North and South Downs.

In or close to the Weald lie a host of pretty villages, handsome towns like Tenterden or Tunbridge Wells, and a great number of attractive country houses, stately homes and public gardens. This is a very pleasant area to visit at any time of year, but since mass market tourism has not yet found a foothold in the Weald, it is especially good in the summertime when the crowds flock to Canterbury or the Kent coast.

Cranbrook is 55 miles from London.

According to the sign outside the church in the town centre, Cranbrook is 'The Capital of the Weald'. It is certainly a very fine town with a self-confident air, and a range of attractions. The most striking of these is the great Union Windmill which overtops the roofs in the middle of the town. Windmills are still fairly common in this part of Kent but the Union Windmill is the largest smock mill in the country, standing over 60ft (18m) high. It was built in 1814 and is still in full working order, the sails turning on windy days to grind out flour which is sold to pay for the mill's upkeep.

Cranbrook is charming, with a wide High Street and lots of smaller lanes lined with half-timbered or white-painted, clapboard houses. The town grew up in the Middle Ages when it became a centre for cloth-weaving, before becoming a market town for the surrounding farms. A good introduction to the area can be found in the Cranbrook Museum near the library, which is full of exhibits on life and industry in the Weald. The great church of St Dunstan stands on the site of a previous Saxon church, and dates from about 1350. Like a number of local churches St Dunstan's is very large and known locally as the 'Cathedral of the Weald'.

On a lighter note, those who browse around Cranbrook, which is a good way to spend a Saturday morning, will soon notice that the town is well supplied with small shops and good pubs. The local people recommend the Prince of Wales, and for good pub food and a wide range of local bitters, the Hooden Horse. The George Hotel in the centre actually did welcome Queen Elizabeth I during one of her progresses through Kent, and Woody's Restaurant in Stone Street serves a very good lunch and, for evening entertainment, jugglers and magicians to perform around the tables.

Stone Street also contains Perfect Partners, an excellent wine and cheese shop. There is a range of over 100, mostly English, cheeses including such

Cranbrook Mill

rare finds as Celtic Promise, Prince Bonnie and Tornegus, many from James Aldridge, doyen of English cheese-makers.

Cranbrook is a good centre for touring the Weald and an ideal base hereabouts is Kennel Holt Hotel, four miles from the town on the road to Goudhurst. The hotel is quite small, with only eight bedrooms, but very beautiful, a manor house built in the Tudor period, with box hedges and topiary in the gardens around the croquet lawn, a large pond and, as a special treat, a warm welcome from Clovis, the giant Schnauzer, who comes lolloping up to greet the guests. The food is excellent and the wine list expansive, the bar in the library operates on the 'sign and pour' honour system and the owners are full of information about the local attractions.

Good hotels are rather rare in the Weald but others worth considering are the Eastwell Manor Hotel at Boughton Aluph near Ashford on the edge of the North Downs, and the Spa Hotel at Tunbridge Wells, a few miles to the west. Eastwell Manor is a luxury hotel set in a 3,000-acre park, and built on the site of a medieval manor.

The Spa Hotel is also set in parkland but within easy walking distance of the Pantiles and the town centre of Tunbridge Wells, and has a health centre and an indoor pool to go with comfortable rooms and good food.

One way to get about and see the area is to follow the waymarks round the High Weald Country Tour, a circular 70-mile-long car route that reaches into every part of the Weald. Although it can be picked up at any point, the tour assumes Tonbridge is the starting point. After a stop at Tonbridge Castle the route leads across the Medway to Hever Castle, once the home of the Boleyns and the place where Henry VIII came to court the Lady Anne, who became his ill-fated second wife. Hever Castle is very beautiful, as is the church of St Peter near the castle gate.

After Hever comes the National Trust village of Chiddingstone, which is full of 16th- and 17th-century houses, and contains the manor house-style Chiddingstone Castle as a central gem. Chiddingstone is especially attractive in the springtime. Then comes Penshurst Place, the splendid home of Lord De L'Isle, where both house and gardens are quite magnificent. The Great Hall at Penshurst dates from the 14th century and the gallery contains portraits of the Sidneys, ancestors of the family who still live here. One of these was the famous Sir Philip Sidney, the Elizabethan soldier poet, and another the late Lord De L'Isle and Dudley, who won the VC at Anzio in 1944.

Penshurst Vineyards, just down the road, are also worth a visit, though this part of Kent is full of vineyards. The largest and most famous is the one at Lamberhurst which produces a wide range of very palatable wines. All these vineyards can be visited and offer tours which end in the vineyard shop. There are more vineyards at Tenterden, Sandhurst, and Biddenden.

Historic country houses and beautiful gardens are the great attractions of a weekend in the Weald. Of all the many gardens the most famous are those at Sissinghurst near Cranbrook; but a word of warning. The tourists know about Sissinghurst and in the summer the place is jammed. Visits here should therefore be made early in the season, in May or in October, before the gardens close for the winter.

One of the lesser known gardens of the Weald is the eight nursery acres of plants, trees and shrubs at Merriments, at Hurst Green near Hawkhurst, just half a mile from the A21. Merriments has a range of over 2,000 plants spanning the seasons.

Another highly recommended garden is Great Dixter near Northiam, south-west of Tenterden. The garden is set about a 15th-century hall restored by Sir Edwin Lutyens for the Lloyd family, who still live there. Sir Edwin also laid out the grounds which include a topiary lawn, with bushes shaped like coffee-pots, a sunken garden and a meadow garden.

Two of the outdoor attractions of the Weald are Bedgebury Pinetum and Bewl Water, both of which are a few miles south of Cranbrook. Bedgebury contains an impressive selection of conifers and is a good place to go walking, with a large number of tracks and trails around the plantation and in the 2,500 acres of Bedgebury Forest which lie alongside.

Bewl Water is a reservoir covering 770 acres. It has canoeing, sailing and fishing, as well as bike rides and walks around the shore. In the spring and autumn a wide variety of waterfowl will interest birdwatchers, and from April to October there are cruises around the lake on the *Frances Mary*, a large steam passenger launch, which offers 'Walk and Cruise' trips and 'Walk and Pub Lunch' cruises.

From Bewl Water it is no distance to Tenterden, a very pretty town, famous for its wide main street and for Smallhythe Place, the home of the actress Ellen Terry, who lived here until her death in 1928. It is now owned by the National Trust and preserved as a memorial to Miss

Terry and such theatrical luminaries as Sir Henry Irving, Mrs Siddons, David Garrick and the rest. Tenterden is also the depot for the Kent and East Sussex Railway, which has steam train excursions across the county border during the summer months.

There is so much to see and do around the Weald of Kent that one visit is barely sufficent to scratch the surface of the area. To the places mentioned here should be added Bodiam Castle in the Rother Valley, and at least half a day should be allowed in Tunbridge Wells for a wander around the Pantiles and a look at the shops.

The villages of Headcorn, Goudhurst, Biddenden and Benenden are also worth a look. Most contain something special to justify the trip, like the aircraft museum at Headcorn Airfield, where a visit can be enlivened by watching the first-time jumpers at the parachute school.

INFORMATION:

CRANBROOK LIES ON THE A229 FROM HAWKHURST TO STAPLEHURST.

KENNEL HOLT HOTEL, TEL. 0580 712032; EASTWELL MANOR HOTEL, BOUGHTON ALUPH, ASHFORD, TEL. 0233 635751; THE SPA HOTEL, TUNBRIDGE WELLS, TEL. 0892 520331. TIC (CRANBROOK), TEL. 0580 712538; TIC (TUNBRIDGE WELLS), TEL. 0892 515675.

13

Dumfries, Galloway and Ayr

—

South of the border, the counties of Dumfries and Galloway would long since have been renamed 'The Robbie Burns Country', but though Burns reminders are everywhere, the local tourist board has resisted that temptation. This seems wise because the area has more to offer than memorials of a long dead but not forgotten poet.

This weekend is spent looking at some of the bountiful offerings of Dumfries and Galloway, though it includes a side trip just across the northern border to Turnberry and the city of Ayr - 'which ne'er a town surpasses, for honest men and bonnie lasses', according to Robert Burns. Dumfries and Turnberry are too far apart to absorb in one weekend, so they should be seen as alternative locations or, better still, as the justification for a second visit to the area.

Dumfries is 80 miles from Edinburgh or Glasgow, 90 miles from Newcastle, and 155 miles from Manchester.

Turnberry is 50 miles from Glasgow, 100 miles from Edinburgh, and 175 miles from Newcastle.

The town of Dumfries, where this weekend begins, lies on the Nith, one of those beautiful but unregarded rivers that flows into the Solway Firth a few miles to the south. Dumfries is known as the 'Queen of the South' and a stroll around the streets will soon reveal why, for Dumfries is splendid. There is Scotland's oldest-surviving (15th-century) multi-arched bridge, which spans the river and has the town's oldest house built at one end. High above that stands the tower of an 18th-century windmill, the top floor of which has a camera obscura, installed in 1836. Through this, projected onto a table-top screen, the visitor can get a moving, panoramic view of the town and the surrounding countryside.

The mill tower houses the Dumfries Museum, the largest in south-west Scotland which, like many of these local museums, contains an eclectic selection of exhibits: stuffed birds from the Solway Firth, tools of prehistoric man, Victorian farm implements, fossils, weapons, stone carvings...something for everyone and very well displayed.

Before returning to the town centre take a look at Dumfries' oldest house, the Old Bridge House, which dates from 1660. This contains another museum with a complete Victorian kitchen, a dentist's surgery and other historical settings of everyday life. Just across the way is St Michael's churchyard where Robert Burns lies buried, having died in Dumfries in 1796. Burns spent the last three years of his life here and his home, now called Burns House, is a place of pilgrimage for lovers of his work.

Dumfries Museum with camera obscura

Visitors can see some of his manuscripts, original letters and many of his personal effects, displayed as though the poet had just gone out for a dram at the Poacher's Rest, a good pub by the river. Rather more up to date is the Robert Burns Centre in Mill Road which uses audio-visual effects to tell the story of the man and his work.

Dumfries and Galloway cover a big area, so there is great scope for car touring in every direction, into the countryside or along the coast. The first direction should be south, to the sandy shores of the Solway Firth, for a look at what remains of Sweetheart Abbey, just beside the A710. The abbey was founded in the 13th century by Devorgilla, Lady of Galloway, in memory of her husband, John de Balliol, who founded Balliol College in Oxford (as a penance for raiding Durham Cathedral). Both Devorgilla and her husband were buried at the abbey, she with the casket in which she kept his embalmed heart. Hence the name.

From here the coast road leads through the Dalbeattie Forest to Castle Douglas, a resort town with a lot to see and do. The National Trust Gardens at Threave are worth a stop, and there are the ruins of Threave Castle on an island in the middle of the Dee. This is one of the oldest sites hereabouts for Castle Douglas itself is not very old, being built in the late 18th century by Sir William Douglas to cater for the local village communities. It has since developed into an artistic centre and supports a great number of potters, glass-blowers, weavers - Galloway tweed is a major export - silk screen printers and painters.

Castle Douglas is one of the stops on the Solway Firth Heritage Trail, which runs along the coast to Stranraer and the Mull of Galloway. To go the full distance would involve driving nearly 200 miles, so I recommend following the A713 northwards along the shores of Loch Ken to the town of New Galloway. Loch Ken is very scenic and New Galloway is a great centre for fishing, birdwatching and walking.

From New Galloway the A712 turns south and west to Newton Stewart, a market town with a long main street, plenty of pubs and a museum depicting local life since the 1750s. Newton Stewart is a woollen centre and those interested in mohair can visit the Creebridge Mills, where the shop has a wide selection of knitwear and tweeds for sale.

North of Newton Stewart lies the vast expanse of the Galloway Forest Park. This area of loch, forest and open hillside contains a great deal of wildlife including red deer, pine martens, otters, feral goats, and birds like the golden eagle and peregrine falcon. Boots and field glasses are essential equipment for a visit there.

The place to start is the Kirroughtree Visitors' Centre near Newton Stewart, which has audio-visual displays on the park wildlife and a number of forest trails to pursue. There are more walks and drives at the Clatteringshaws Forest Wildlife Centre, five miles up the A712.

The park covers 290 square miles and could take a week to explore, not least because there are a lot of historic sites, some of which can only be seen on foot. At Bruce's Stone in Glen Trool, a magnificent valley near Newton Stewart, Robert the Bruce won an early victory over the English in the war of independence. From Glen Trool, which lies on the route of the South Uplands Way, there is a stiff climb to the top of Merrick mountain, at 2,764ft (842m) the highest peak in southern Scotland; there is also a four-mile walk along the shores of Loch Trool.

North of Newton Stewart the road crosses the border into Ayrshire and the South Uplands Way, one of Scotland's long-distance footpaths, which runs for 212 miles, from Stranraer to the Firth of Forth near Edinburgh. It is well waymarked and can be easily followed here for a mile or so across the hills. The Way from Loch Trool to Bargrennan is just seven and a half miles, a good walk through wonderful country.

Pressing north, the road reaches the coast again at Girvan, 20 miles south of Ayr. Between Girvan and Ayr is the second place worthy of a weekend visit in this part of south-west Scotland, the golf course and hotel at Turnberry. The links at Turnberry attract championship competitions and golfers from all over the world, for the golf is challenging and the courses lie in a spectacular setting, with the rock of Ailsa Craig jutting out of the Firth offshore and the hotel hovering on the hillside behind.

The Turnberry Hotel now has a health spa offering day rates to passing travellers, so one partner can pass the time here while the other plays golf. The craggy island of Ailsa Craig, the peak of a long extinct volcano and now a bird sanctuary, can be visited from Girvan.

Ayr is another centre for the Robert Burns industry and contains the Auld Kirk, built in 1654, where the poet was baptised and sometimes worshipped, and the Tam o' Shanter Museum from where his cheerful drunk set out on his famous ride on Meg, his 'auld grey mare', with the witch Cutty Sark in hot pursuit. There is the Tam o' Shanter pub in the town centre and at Alloway, a suburb of Ayr, the cottage where Burns was born on 25 January 1759 - 'Burns Night', a date celebrated by Scots in every corner of the world. There are also many castles, like the splendid one at Culzean just south of Ayr, built by Robert Adam in the 18th century and now owned by the National Trust for Scotland.

After the last war the people of Scotland offered General - later President - Dwight Eisenhower a lifetime's lease on an apartment at Culzean, and the castle contains a fascinating Eisenhower Exhibition depicting Ike's career in war and peace. Culzean was Scotland's first country park and the attractions include woodland walks, a forestry exhibition, three miles of rugged coastline and a deer park.

Dumfries and Galloway and the coast of Ayr are too big to be seen in one weekend, but those who enjoy the plentiful attractions are sure to come back.

INFORMATION:

DUMFRIES LIES ON THE A75 ANNAN TO CASTLE DOUGLAS ROAD, AT THE JUNCTION WITH THE A709 WEST FROM LOCKERBIE.

TURNBERRY IS ON THE WEST COAST AT THE JUNCTION OF THE A77 NORTH FROM GIRVAN AND THE A719 SOUTH FROM AYR.

THE CAIRNDALE HOTEL, DUMFRIES, TEL. 0387 54111; THE URR VALLEY COUNTRY HOUSE HOTEL, CASTLE DOUGLAS, TEL. 0556 2188; THE TURNBERRY HOTEL AND SPA, TURNBERRY, TEL. 0655 310000. TIC (DUMFRIES), TEL. 0387 53862; TIC (AYR), TEL. 0292 284196.

14

Ely and the Fens

—

Britain is full of interesting towns, many of them cathedral cities, places where there is a lot to do within the confines and plenty to see in the countryside round about. Just such a place is Ely, 17 miles north of Cambridge and close to the haunting country of the East Anglian Fens. In the winter this part of England can be damp and bleak, but during the other seasons of the year it is a place to savour.

Ely is 80 miles from London, 110 miles from Birmingham, and 150 miles from Leeds.

The area around Ely is flat, so flat that the city's great cathedral, 'The Cathedral of the Fens', stands out above the surrounding countryside, riding the green surface of the marshland like a great stone ship. Part of this must be due to the fact that in Fenland terms Ely occupies a mountain, all of 70ft (21m) high, which lifts the town above the flood plain of the River Ouse. The story of this plain is part of the history of Ely and the Fen country.

Until the 17th century the Fens were little more than a marshy swamp. Then the Earl of Bedford hired a Dutch engineer, Cornelius Vermuyden, to drain the marshes and create ground fit for agriculture. This he did; the land was retrieved from the waters and the levels fell, until today ground level in the Fen country is many feet below what it was three centuries ago. Ely, the Fenland capital, therefore stands supreme.

Ely is an old town and this shows in the narrow streets and walled gardens around the cathedral. The Danes sacked Ely in AD870 and after the Conquest Hereward the Wake, the last Saxon still in arms, made one final, desperate, unavailing stand here against the Norman invader.

The cathedral began to go up in 1083, but as so often happened with medieval cathedrals, parts of it later fell down and had to be rebuilt. What stands today is a medieval masterpiece, with towers rather than spires and a magnificent interior with splendid choir stalls and wonderful vaulting in the choir.

There are plenty of other old buildings in Ely and a stroll around the back streets and down to the river will reveal a varied collection of architecture and some fine walled gardens, but after the cathedral the next stop - or stops - should be on the Palace Green. The first is at the Tourist Information Centre, next to St Mary's church, which apart from dispensing lots of useful information on the area was the home of Oliver Cromwell from 1636 to 1646.

The staff of the TIC offer a guided tour around several of the rooms which are furnished in contemporary 17th-century style, as well as showing a video of Cromwell's life. There is another video on the story of the Fens, a useful preliminary to a tour of the area.

Across the way from the tourist centre is the Doll's House Atelier, a

Oliver Cromwell's house

small shop which sells dolls' houses and all that they contain - from Tudor four-posters to a state-of-the-art jacuzzi.

The next stop, since lunchtime must be approaching, is at the Old Fire Engine House on the green, set in a former farmhouse built in 1614, and the place where the town's fire engine was kept at the turn of the century. This is one of those unusual restaurants where the way to the dining room is through the kitchen. Another rare touch is a total absence of portion control; those who finish their steak and kidney pie or vegetable moussaka will be offered a second helping.

After lunch some further strolling might be advisable, to see the monastic buildings around the King's School, or along the local town footpath - the Bishop's Way - which runs past the cathedral; or down to the Ouse where the river cruisers moor after the trip up from Cambridge. River cruisers can be hired for the day in Ely or Cambridge and used to sail up or down the Ouse between the two cities.

Accommodation in Ely tends to be limited. The Lamb Hotel on Lynn Road, once a coaching inn, is right on the corner by the traffic lights, so a room overlooking the car park might be advisable. Otherwise visitors might prefer to stay in Cambridge or in Newmarket.

Once Ely has been explored, a task which will take about half a day, there is time to seek out other attractions round about. Cambridge is always worth a look, even by those who know it well, or you can drive out to the pretty villages of Grantchester and Trumpington, though these tend to be somewhat crowded on a summer weekend.

Cambridge is too well known to need further explanation here, but just 13 miles from Ely is the somewhat less familiar town of Newmarket, a place largely devoted to the horse. At any one time there will be some 2,500 racehorses in training here, continuing a tradition that goes back to the time of Charles II. The story of British horse-racing can be exhaustively researched in Newmarket at the National Stud, especially in the springtime when foals seem to be scampering everywhere, and the National Horseracing Museum, or at a meeting on the local racecourse.

Ely is an excellent touring centre for North Cambridgeshire and the Fens and there are two tours, one on foot, one by car, that will give the visitor a good insight into this fascinating region.

To explore the local area on foot follow The Bishop's Way, a 7-9 mile circular, waymarked walk north of the city, that can begin by the cathedral and is easily traced using an illustrated leaflet available from the TIC. The Way follows the path used by the Bishop to reach his palace at Downham, just to the north.

From the cathedral the Way runs out of the town and in to the Fens along Clayway Drove, a cattle trail above the marshes to Chettisham, which was listed in 1170 as a local parish. This is an easy, if muddy, route through country created by the draining of the Fens. The ever-attendant birds and butterflies, and the local flora of bullrushes and cowslips, are quite delightful. The path wanders along for four miles into Downham, a small village, built like Ely on a mound of clay and gravel set above the plain. Downham has a couple of good pubs, The Anchor and The Plough, both handy for lunch or a drink before walking round the last half of the Way and back towards the towers of Ely Cathedral.

The second way to explore the Fen country is by following the Dorothy L.Sayers Trail, across the Fens to Downham Market, 20 miles to the north. This, too, is the subject of an illustrated leaflet from the Ely TIC and takes in places featured by the writer in her thrillers, in particular those graced by that aristocrat of detectives, Lord Peter Wimsey.

Dorothy L.Sayers lived at Bluntisham, 10 miles south-west of Ely, and the trail runs from there to March, a small town where the church of St Wendreda was one of several which inspired her book, *The Nine Tailors*. Take a look in this church, if only for the wonderful hammer-beam roof. Dorothy's father was the rector of Christchurch, a village just to the east, down the B1099, which has a memorial in the vestry. From here the route runs on to two villages, Upwell and Outwell, and if they both look like transplants from Holland this is because Dutch engineers who came to advise on how to drain the Fens stayed long enough to influence the local builders.

Wisbech is a fine town, a former port with a Saturday market. From there follow signs to Walpole St Peter, which was used as the setting for *The Nine Tailors* in the BBC TV series. Then comes Downham Market, another pleasant little town, and so down the A10 back to Ely, where we began.

Both these tours have a theme but are really just good ways to see a little more of this flat country and marvel at the effort that has gone into creating it. The work of draining the Fens has gone on since Roman times, and still continues. The Romans dug the Car Dyke, 70 miles long, partly to drain the waters and partly to create a canal which would carry supplies to the garrison at Lincoln in the north. At one time the Fen country had over 2,000 windmills, each engaged in pumping out the water; many of these remain, some complete with sails, a picturesque sight in an otherwise unremarkable landscape.

INFORMATION:

ELY LIES ON THE A10 BETWEEN CAMBRIDGE AND DOWNHAM MARKET, AT THE JUNCTION WITH THE A142 FROM NEWMARKET.

LAMB HOTEL, ELY, TEL. 0353 663574; FENLAND LODGE HOTEL, STUNTNEY, NEAR ELY, TEL. 0353 667047; SWYNFORD PADDOCKS HOTEL, SIX MILE BOTTOM, NEWMARKET, TEL. 063870 234. TIC (ELY), TEL. 0353 662062.

15

Forest of Dean

—

The Forest of Dean remains one of the more mysterious parts of Britain. Until the motorways forged across the Severn, the Forest of Dean was a quiet backwater west of the river, inhabited by iron workers and coal miners, small farmers and a great quantity of sheep. The hills and valleys of the Forest remain remote, bleak in winter, glorious in all the other seasons of the year.

The Forest of Dean is 30 miles from Bristol, 40 miles from Cardiff, 70 miles from Birmingham, and 130 miles from London.

The Forest of Dean lies just across the Severn from the southern slopes of the Cotswolds, but no two areas could be more different. Where the villages of the Cotswolds are uniform and charming, those of the Forest of Dean are a jumble of houses and workmen's cottages, somewhat short of architectural appeal.

Where the slopes of the Cotswolds are open and airy, the main feature of the Forest is the great oak woods, blanketed with bluebells in May, glorious in their autumn foliage. The Forest is not a managed area, though it is now controlled by the Forestry Commission. It has been a National Park since 1938 but is still a real forest, dating back to the Norman Conquest. It is correctly called the Royal Forest of Dean, with a charter from William the Conqueror, who decreed that anyone felling a tree or hunting in the Forest without his express permission would be mutilated.

The Forest oaks once provided timber to the Royal Navy and although quite small, covering just 35 miles, the Forest remains one of the finest woodland areas in Britain, a place well worth exploring by car, on foot or by bicycle.

First though, where to stay. There are a number of good hotels, in or around the Forest, but the prime destination is the Speech House Hotel at Coleford. The Speech House is right in the centre of the Forest, opposite a marker which confirms this fact, and the starting point for numerous walks into the woods. This building, erected in 1680, was built to house the Court of Verderers, the officials who control the Forest for the Crown, and still meet twice a year in the dining room of the hotel. Established in 1017 by a charter of King Canute, the Court of Verderers is the oldest court of law in the United Kingdom.

The Speech House can boast many Royal connections. Charles II brought Nell Gwynne here for the weekend, and our present Queen attended a session of the Court of Verderers soon after her coronation in 1953.

It can be seen that the Speech House is no ordinary hotel, but a house of character. It is quite small, but the rooms are comfortable and well furnished - one with a 7ft x 7ft (2m x 2m) four-poster - and the food in the restaurant draws people from all over the area. As you would expect, the staff are a mine of information on the Forest.

One of the first things to do in the Forest is to go for a walk. Several walks begin right outside the hotel, including a six-mile tramp to Blakeney, or the even longer eight miles to St Briavels; or, for something shorter, the four-mile-round walk to Cannop Ponds. Close to Cannop Ponds is Russells Inclosure, the very heart of the old forest. The enclosure was listed as long ago as 1282 and is much as it was then, a wilderness seamed with small paths.

All these walks are a marvellous way to explore the Forest. Some of them are even better at certain times of the year, like the Daffodil Way in the Vale of Leadon to the north-west, which runs through a carpet of daffodils in springtime. The Vale of Leadon is a beautiful place, set with pretty villages full of black-and-white timbered houses, typical of the Welsh Marches.

Another, more curious walk, is the four-mile-long Sculpture Trail which begins at the Beechenhurst Lodge picnic site off the B4226, and leads to sculptures set in the woods, each illustrating some aspect of life in the Forest. Some of these are quite remarkable, like the Cathedral sculpture where a stained-glass window is suspended at the end of a nave of trees. Other sculptures, alas, have already been vandalised, but this is a walk no visitor should miss.

A good way to gain an understanding of the Forest is to visit the Dean Heritage Centre at Soudley, five miles from the Speech House, and set in and around an old watermill. This aims to display the ancient life of the Royal Forest, illustrating the work of the iron, coal and stone miners, the foresters and shepherds. It is all very well done, with a charcoal burners' camp, a smithy, craft workshops, and various nature trails - for the Forest is a marvellous habitat for wildlife.

Walking is a major activity for visitors to the Forest, but those people who are not interested in foot-powered travel will still find plenty to enjoy. Lovers of the curious are particularly well looked after, especially at Littledean Hall at Cinderford, which is said to be one of the most haunted houses in England. Ghost sightings are rare these days, but the display of crocus in the early spring is a sight to see.

South of here the Severn narrows to sweep round the curve at Newnham, and this is a good place to see the famous Severn Bore, a six-foot-high (2m) tidal wave that comes sweeping up the river in the spring and autumn; the local people are authorities on the Bore and can advise visitors when it is likely to appear.

For railway buffs there is the Great Western Railway Museum at

Drift mine, Forest of Dean

Coleford, while steam train lovers should not miss a ride on the Dean Forest Railway from the town of Lydney on the bank of the Severn, north to Norchard. Do not leave Lydney without visiting the Lydney Park Gardens, which are a blaze of rhododendrons and azaleas in the spring. Since the Forest is not very large, confined by three rivers and laced with roads and lanes, it is easy to get about and quite hard to get lost. A good tour might begin at Chepstow, an old town which has a popular racecourse and a very splendid castle, and stands astride the Offa's Dyke footpath. Once inside the 16th-century gate, the town falls away down the hillside to the Wye.

A few miles away lie the ruins of Tintern Abbey, immortalised by Wordsworth. Then comes Monmouth, the birthplace of Henry V, which contains a museum on Admiral Horatio Nelson. Visitors who cannot get into the Speech House might try the King's Head Hotel in Agincourt Square. Then comes Symonds Yat, a popular spot on the Wye with wonderful views over the river, and the Symonds Yat Maze in Jubilee Park; this maze is newer than the one at Hampton Court but great fun.

The Wye Valley at Symonds Yat is beautiful enough to justify its popularity. The attractions and lure of the Forest of Dean are less easy to define but lie in the remoter parts, along those walks and rides deep among the fir and oak trees, away from the summer crowds along the river.

Within the Forest the main crowds are provided by the sheep, which appear everywhere and seem fond of dozing against the stone walls and kerbstones by the side of the road. The Forest of Dean is a very special area, a historic part of Britain, a place apart. There is not a lot of nightlife aside from the pubs, but otherwise there is much to see and do; though the real appeal of this ancient region lies in that timeless air that is difficult to find anywhere else nowadays but seems to exist here, under the great canopy of trees.

INFORMATION:

THE FOREST OF DEAN LIES EAST OF THE A466 BETWEEN CHEPSTOW AND MONMOUTH, WEST OF THE A48 FROM GLOUCESTER TO CHEPSTOW.

THE SPEECH HOUSE HOTEL, COLEFORD, TEL. 0594 822607; THE CORSE LAWN HOUSE HOTEL, FORTHAMPTON, TEL. 0452 780479; KING'S HEAD HOTEL, MONMOUTH, TEL. 0600 712177. TIC (COLEFORD), TEL. 0594 836307; TIC (GLOUCESTER), TEL. 0452 421188.

16

Goring and Streatley

—

The twin villages of Goring and Streatley lie on either side of the Thames, at the point where the river forces a path through the Chiltern escarpment at the Goring Gap. With a mixture of riverside and wooded hills, two good hotels, several friendly pubs, good walks along the river and the city of Oxford in easy reach, this delightful corner of the Thames Valley is perfect for an impromptu weekend.

Goring is 55 miles from London, and 90 miles from Bristol or Birmingham.

Goring and Streatley are separate places, each with its own church, pubs and distinctive architecture, but they ought to be taken as a whole. Along the green length of the Thames Valley they are referred to as 'Goring 'n' Streatley' anyway, and since they are only separated by a river bridge and a hundred yards of road it seems pointless to be pedantic. Take them together and enjoy the lot, Goring on the north bank and Streatley on the south.

They mark the site of a major ford across the Thames and if the villages are relatively recent in Thames Valley terms, having medieval roots and 18th-century architecture, there has been traffic through

Streatley on Thames

this spot since prehistoric times. The Thames broke through the Chiltern Hills here way back in the Ice Age, and when the ice melted and life was restored, two long tracks - the motorways of pre-history - used the Goring Gap as a passing point: the Icknield Way coming from the north, and the Ridgeway leading south across the Berkshire Downs.

This point is still relevant because that modern walkers' route, the 80-mile-long Ridgeway footpath, comes down to the Gap off the Chiltern escarpment and leads up Streatley Hill, and after another 40 miles or so to Amesbury, sticking more or less to the prehistoric route.

Many of these long-distance walkers overnight in Goring 'n' Streatley, no doubt some of them in the youth hostel by the Reading road, but others in more glitzy accommodation. The villages can offer two hotels, the Swan Diplomat in Streatley and the Miller of Mansfield in Goring.

The Swan Diplomat is an elegant four-star riverside hotel by Goring lock, with its own moorings. The gardens are beautiful, ideal for an evening stroll or a breath of air before breakfast.

Across the river, in the centre of Goring, the red-brick Miller of Mansfield is smaller, older and often noisier, with just 10 bedrooms. Half-pub, half-hotel, very popular with local people and walkers on the Ridgeway Path, the Miller of Mansfield, or something just like it, has stood on this spot opposite the church since the Norman Conquest.

The name is curious and is said to date from the reign of King John. The king was on a visit to Mansfield in the Midlands where the local miller served him a dish of venison. The meal was delicious but it then occurred to the king that since hunting deer was a royal prerogative, the venison must have been stolen. Though not normally benign, the king decided not to hang the miller, provided he moved to Goring and served just such a meal every time the king rode past from London to Oxford. All rubbish, of course, since King John died in 1216 and the present inn is much later, but a good tale is worth telling and the food at the Miller of Mansfield is still very good.

The best way to enjoy Goring and Streatley is on foot. The parking is terrible and both hotels are no distance from the local sights, chief of which is Goring Lock, a short stroll from either hotel. I can think of no better way to unwind after a hard week's work and the drive down from London or the Midlands, than by sitting on the lawns by Goring Lock watching the boats and cabin cruisers go through on a summer evening.

Watch the boats for a while, then stroll about the villages, which contain a great many worthwhile examples of domestic architecture. Nip into the churches if they are open - the church of St Thomas à Becket in Goring has a bell dating from 1290, one of the oldest in England. Other buildings to take in are Goring Mill by the bridge, and the village hall in Streatley which was once the old malt house.

The scenery around the Goring Gap is varied and, in a very English way, rather spectacular. It is certainly very beautiful, especially in the early morning when the mist is still rising from the river. Just to the north lie the Chiltern beechwoods, a 300-square mile Area of Outstanding Natural Beauty, glorious in the autumn, when the beech leaf is on the turn, but almost equally attractive at every other season of the year.

To the south, after a rather puffing one-hour climb on the waymarked Ridgeway Path to the top of Streatley Hill, the open, airy Berkshire Downs appear, with vast views under a canopy of sky. On either side lies the river valley, a patchwork of fields and copses, dotted with small hamlets and riverside villages, many of which can be visited on foot.

The local paths can be muddy so take walking shoes or boots. Good walks include anywhere along the Thames towpath, the Goring to Gatehampton walk through the Great Chalk Wood, which is a good morning stroll, or the one-hour walk to the gardens and bird park of the Childe Beale Trust at nearby Basildon. For something shorter with a definite objective at the end, there is the walk to Basildon Park, a National Trust property off the Reading road. This is the most splendid Georgian house in Berkshire, built by John Carr of York in 1776, and used in World War II as the headquarters for the American Airborne. Virtually derelict by the early 1950s, it has since been immaculately restored and has wonderful gardens.

If the weather is unkind, or unsuitable for walking, don't worry. Goring and Streatley have something to offer in all weathers and in any season of the year, and the villages round about are well worth exploring. Pangbourne, a few miles south-east down the Reading road, is a pretty spot with cafés and antique shops and one very good restaurant at the Copper Inn. Pangbourne is famous for its Nautical College and for the fact that this is where Kenneth Grahame lived while writing *Wind in the Willows*, so lovers of Mole and Ratty will want to make a pilgrimage.

Up on the Berkshire Downs lies Wantage, the ancient capital of Wessex and once the home of King Alfred, whose statue stands in the market square. Wantage is a small, attractive market town surrounded by villages full of racing stables. Villages worth a stop include Aldworth, where the church contains the tombs of the Aldworth Giants, the mighty men of the de la Beche family, soldiers of the Black Prince. The yew tree outside Aldworth church is one of the oldest in the country, estimated as having stood there for around 1,000 years.

Further up the river lie a score of pretty places within a short drive. I recommend Dorchester-on-Thames, which has another well-known hostelry, The George, several antique shops for a good browse, and Dorchester Abbey, which is an unusual mixture of Norman and Gothic architecture and has some interesting windows.

Ewelme, a small flower-filled hamlet set above watercress beds near the larger village and airfield at Benson, is a late medieval gem in rose-red brick. Most of the village was built by the Duke and Duchess of Suffolk in the 15th century. The village school they erected is still in use, as are the almshouses in the cloisters of the little Gothic church, which contains marvellously emblazoned tombs and an alabaster effigy of the duchess.

A weekend in Goring and Streatley provides a range of delights, while those who want a little excitement or a city for a rainy day have Oxford, with its shops, cinemas, theatres and colleges, just a few miles up the road.

INFORMATION:

THE VILLAGES OF GORING AND STREATLEY LIE ON THE A329 FROM READING TO WALLINGFORD.

THE SWAN DIPLOMAT HOTEL, STREATLEY, TEL. 0491 873737; THE MILLER OF MANSFIELD, GORING, TEL. 0491 872829. TIC (WALLINGFORD), TEL. 0491 26972.

17

Helmsley and Ryedale

—

Helmsley is one of the smaller towns of Yorkshire, yet a place with a great deal to offer. Close to the city of York, just below the Yorkshire Moors and with plenty of attractions in the district of Ryedale round about, this charming little market town makes a good centre for a weekend break.

Helmsley is 50 miles from Leeds, 75 miles from Newcastle, 100 miles from Manchester, and 165 miles from Birmingham.

Ryedale is not small; it covers some 600 square miles of country south of the North Yorkshire Moors and north of the Wolds, an area full of attractive villages, stately homes and famous abbeys, with lots of outdoor activities ranging from good walks to golf, fishing and rides on the North Yorkshire Moors Railway.

I have selected Helmsley partly because it is quieter than the more obvious centres like Malton and Pickering, partly because it has a castle, and partly because it lies close to the romantic ruins of Rievaulx Abbey. It also has the Black Swan Hotel, looking out on the old buildings surrounding the market square which occupies the centre of the town. The Black Swan was an Elizabethan coaching inn, but has expanded over the years to embrace a Tudor rectory, a Georgian house and some pleasant gardens.

Helmsley is well worth exploring, with a number of attractive streets and alleyways and one or two good pubs like the Faversham Arms in the market square. Just above the square stands the gaunt ruins of Helmsley Castle, which dates back to Norman times and was destroyed during the Civil War.

A stroll to Helmsley Castle is one of the walks ideal before dinner, but there are plenty of others and the town stands on the junction of two long-distance footpaths, the Ebor Way and the Cleveland Way. The Cleveland Way starts in Helmsley and runs for 108 miles to Filey Brig on the Yorkshire coast. Good local walks include the two-hour tramp to the White Horse on Sutton Bank which, apart from being the only White Horse in Yorkshire, has marvellous views over Ryedale. Another good walk is the one to Rievaulx Abbey, which could occupy Sunday morning.

Temple, Rievaulx Abbey

Rievaulx Abbey is quite beautiful, a tragedy in stone, though part of the ruins have been restored and the Ionic Temple in the grounds, which was built by a local landowner, Thomas Duncombe, in the 18th century, is now a restaurant. Rievaulx is a Cistercian foundation, one of the many which once littered Yorkshire, built from 1131 by Walter d'Espec, the lord of Helmsley Castle. The abbey flourished throughout the Middle Ages and then came Henry VIII's Reformation; lovely Rievaulx Abbey was destroyed and the community dispersed.

The abbey then came into the possession of the Duncombes of Duncombe Park, now the home of Lord and Lady Faversham. Duncombe was built in 1713, and though damaged by fire at the end of the last century, has been wonderfully restored. With its 18th-century landscaped gardens, woodland walks and views across the Rye Valley, Duncombe Park is a fine place to explore on a warm summer day; as is Byland Abbey, another Cistercian monastery, a few miles south of Helmsley off the road to Thirsk.

Helmsley could occupy an entire weekend, but Ryedale ought to be explored. There is a circular tour through Pickering and Malton which takes in most of the major attractions, so take the A170 for Pickering, turning left after about six miles for the village of Hutton-le-Hole. Pretty Hutton-le-Hole contains the Ryedale Folk Museum, a collection of historic buildings displaying a thousand years of rural history.

Pickering is a town with two claims to fame, one ancient and one modern. The former is the medieval wall paintings in the parish church of St Peter and St Paul, probably the finest in the country; the latter is the North Yorkshire Moors Railway, which runs north from Pickering for 18 miles to Grosmont.

This is a line with history for it was built by the Father of Railways, George Stephenson, and was one of the world's first passenger lines. The line runs through the North Yorkshire Moors National Park, through some of the most beautiful scenery in the county, so a trip on it is not to be missed.

At Pickering our route turns south across the Vale of Pickering for Malton. Most Yorkshire towns have medieval roots but Malton existed before the Romans came, when it became the garrison town of Derventio. The long history of this pleasant market town is shown in the Malton Museum. There is a Saturday market and good lunches at the Green Man Hotel in the town centre, and it is said that Charles Dickens, who often visited Malton, used the town as background for *A Christmas Carol*. Malton hosts a Dickens' Festival every Christmas to celebrate the connection.

Apart from these three market towns, Ryedale is full of pleasant villages, many with something special to offer. Hovingham, six miles south of Helmsley, has a lot of agreeable rural architecture and the Malt Shovel, a country pub with a particularly good dining room; Slingsby, just beyond Hovingham on the B1257, is an old village, part-Saxon, part-Danish, with a ruined castle and a maypole on the green.

South of Slingsby stands Castle Howard, which gained fame in the 1980s as the setting for the television version of Evelyn Waugh's *Brideshead Revisited*. Castle Howard is a splendid house, built at the start of the 18th century by the 3rd Earl of Carlisle to designs prepared by Sir John Vanbrugh, the architect of Blenheim Palace. Another notable architect, Nicholas Hawksmoor, took over the work later, but the Earl and both his architects died before the building was completed. The gardens are superb, the house contains a vast collection of treasures, and a tour of Castle Howard should form part of any visit to Ryedale.

Something rather less usual is Eden Camp, off the A169 north of Malton. Eden Camp was a Second World War prisoner-of-war camp holding Italian and German POWs. According to the tourist board, a number of former inmates are returning to see the camp and more of the local countryside than was available to them in 1939-45. The camp is in a good state of preservation and has been turned into a museum covering just about every aspect of the war, with exhibits on things like the London Blitz, the U-boat menace, bomber operations and, of course, the life of a POW.

Most of all though, Ryedale is an area to roam about on foot or by car, choosing minor roads whenever possible. There are places worth seeing in every corner of the district and no need to follow a fixed itinerary; just mark a few locations on a good road map and wander.

Places that merit a visit include Kirbymoorside, east of Helmsley, a market town, with cobbled streets, a ruined castle, the 15th-century church of All Saints, and the Black Swan pub which dates from the 16th century. Up on the moors nearby lie other attractive places like the villages of Cropton and Lastingham. Just go to Ryedale and tour about; wherever your travels take you, you will not be disappointed.

INFORMATION:

HELMSLEY LIES ON THE A170 MIDWAY BETWEEN PICKERING AND THIRSK.

THE BLACK SWAN, HELMSLEY, TEL. 0439 70466; THE GREEN MAN HOTEL, MALTON, TEL. 0653 600370. TIC (HELMSLEY), TEL. 0439 70173; TIC (PICKERING), TEL. 0751 73791.

18

Hurstbourne Tarrant and the Wessex Downs

—

The Wessex Downs are one of those out-of-the-way places of the English countryside. In the triangle that runs from Newbury to Lambourn, south to St Mary Bourne and Highclere, lies an area of great natural beauty containing every traveller's dream of rural England: unspoilt villages, nice pubs, good walks and a surprising number of things to see and do.

Hurstbourne Tarrant is 75 miles from London, 80 miles from Bristol, and 110 miles from Birmingham.

Hurstbourne Tarrant is a tiny place, with a church and a couple of pubs. Where it scores is in the surrounding countryside and its proximity to the market town of Newbury and the M4 motorway. The suggested base for this weekend is the Esseborne Manor Hotel, 10 miles south of Newbury, a friendly, country house hotel, where family photographs are littered about the public rooms.

For exercise and local entertainment the hotel has an all-weather tennis court and a croquet lawn, and can also offer clay pigeon shooting and golf; but the range of local activities and interests extends well beyond the hotel boundary. An excellent guide book to the local walks and car tours can be found in every bedroom.

The restaurant at Esseborne Manor features a very English menu, with things like Cornish scallops for dinner and only English cheese on the cheeseboard, including a local Newbury goats' cheese.

From Esseborne the surrounding area is in easy reach on quiet roads, or on a network of local footpaths. Some of these paths are part of longer trails like the Wayfarer's Walk, an 80-mile footpath from the Wessex Downs to the Solent, which runs a mile or so north of the hotel.

There are shorter, one-hour walks to Hurstbourne Tarrant, or around the scattering of hamlets and villages, each with a good friendly pub which can serve as the focus for any footpath expedition.

People who, like me, prefer a walk with a theme, can follow the Test Way for a mile or so, or walk up to Combe Gibbet for fantastic views over the surrounding countryside. People who love bunnies can hardly miss a walk on Watership Down which lies east of the A34, five miles south of Newbury.

There are good pubs everywhere offering snacks, coffee, keg bitter and a chance to rest the feet. These include The Fox at Tangley, The Hamster at Hatherden, The Jack Russell at Faccombe and The Plough at Ashmansworth.

Another pub which would offer a little light relief on some gentle towpath walking is the Dundas Arms at Kintbury, a very pretty village on the Kennet and Avon Canal, 10 miles north of Hurstbourne Tarrant. These establishments all offer good pub grub, but for something a little special try the Yew Tree at Hollington Cross on the Andover road near Highclere, which has a good line in country sausages.

Another way to explore the delightful Kennet and Avon Canal from Kintbury is with an excursion on a horse-drawn barge, currently drawn by Queenie, who pulls the barge along sedately, as horses did when the Kennet and Avon was a busy commercial waterway.

The Kennet and Avon towpath would provide a good excursion for couples where only one wants to walk. For example, one could try the six-mile Kintbury-to-Newbury towpath walk, where the return journey or a meeting at the far end can be made by local train.

For couples where one member actually

Barge decoration

detests walking there are a number of suggestions, including a visit to the Inglewood Health Hydro. The Inglewood 'Look Lovely' day includes beauty treatments, a facial, swimming and jacuzzi sessions, lunch and a hair-do, and will return the guest to Esseborne Manor, after a long day of pampering.

This is also a wonderful area for anyone interested in horses. The villages of the Berkshire Downs to the north of Newbury are full of racing stables. The village of Lambourn offers a tour of the local racing stables, and there are regular meetings on the Newbury course featuring both flat racing and 'over the sticks'.

As for excursions to the local sights, where to start? A good place might be at Highclere Castle, five miles south of Newbury on the A34. Highclere Castle is the home of Lord and Lady Carnarvon, and if the house is open to view, which it is throughout the summer and on most weekends, it should certainly not be missed.

The house is a mixture of Gothic and Italianate styles, blended together by Sir Charles Barry, architect of the Houses of Parliament. Highclere was completed in 1842, though on the site of another house, the grounds of which were designed by Capability Brown.

The gardens at Highclere are magnificent, containing a Victorian tropical conservatory where grapefruit, figs and oranges grow alongside bananas and coffee plants.

The house has a vast library, also designed by Sir Charles Barry, with more than 7,000 books, and as a particular gem, a desk which once belonged to Napoleon Bonaparte. There is a portrait of Charles I by Van Dyck in the dining room and a large number of Egyptian relics, recalling the fact that it was the present Earl's grandfather, the 5th Earl, who funded those digs of Howard Carter in the Valley of the Kings which led to the discovery of the tomb of Tutankhamen. If Highclere Castle looks somewhat familier on a first visit, this may be because it has provided the location for some episodes in the *Jeeves and Wooster* TV series.

If Highclere is closed or the weather unkind, there is plenty of interest in and around the market town of Newbury. For a spot of shopping there is the Kennet Centre, with over 50 shops and major stores. For a little more exercise on a wet day there is the Northcroft Recreation Centre, which has swimming pools, a sauna and solarium, and a health suite and fitness studio; while for some evening entertainment there is the small but excellent Watermill Theatre at Bagnor.

Newbury is an old town with Saxon roots and a lot of history. During the English Civil War it was the site of two battles, and some relics of those violent days still remain - at Donnington Castle, two miles north of the town, which was beseiged during the war, and at Littlecote House, 10 miles to the west near Hungerford.

Littlecote House is a splendid Tudor pile, set in 100 acres of ground, containing the finest collection of Civil War arms and armour in England. The house also hosts a summer-long series of special events, including falconry and an annual balloon festival.

Do not leave Newbury without a visit to the Newbury District Museum, which now occupies the former Cloth Hall. The cloth trade was important here in the 15th century, and one of the local characters in the 18th century was weaver John Winchcombe, or 'Jack o' Newbury', who made a coat from sheeps' back to customer's back in the fast time of 13 hours and 20 minutes, a record which stood until 1991. The current record-holding Newbury Coat is one of the prize exhibits in the District Museum, which has a number of fascinating displays.

The Stanley Spencer Great War memorial chapel at Burghclere, off the A34 south of Newbury, is something else to see. There are herb gardens at Hollington near Highclere and rainforest plant life at Wyld Court in Hampstead Norreys, and Hungerford seven miles west of Newbury is stuffed with antique shops. All in all, there is plenty to occupy the visitor to the gentle countryside of the Wessex Downs.

INFORMATION:

HURSTBOURNE TARRANT LIES ON THE A343 BETWEEN NEWBURY AND ANDOVER, AT THE JUNCTION WITH THE B3048.

ESSEBORNE MANOR HOTEL, HURSTBOURNE TARRANT, TEL. 026476 444; INGLEWOOD HEALTH HYDRO, KINTBURY, TEL. 0488 682022; THE CHEQUERS, NEWBURY, TEL. 0635 38000. TIC (NEWBURY), TEL. 0635 30267; TIC (ANDOVER), TEL. 0264 324320.

19

Kelso and the Borders

—

The Cheviot Hills and the Valley of the Tweed define the Scottish Border, a region of smooth hills and rushing rivers, rich in scenery and history. There is a great deal to see and do here for those prepared to poke down minor roads and learn a little of their country's past, whether that country be England or Scotland.

The weekend is based on the town of Kelso, but takes in a lot of places along this embattled frontier. This Border countryside is little known, but there are plenty of attractions and the weather is nowhere near as bad as people might suppose.

Kelso is 50 miles from Edinburgh, 65 miles from Newcastle, 90 miles from Glasgow, and 155 miles from Leeds.

Kelso lies on the Tweed, and according to Sir Walter Scott, is 'the most beautiful, if not the most romantic town in Scotland'. The town grew up around Kelso Abbey, founded by the Scottish monarch David I in 1128. King David lived in the nearby castle of Roxburgh and his monastic foundation became a seat of Scottish learning, in spite of the Border wars which disrupted the contemplative life at frequent intervals.

Kelso Abbey was destroyed in the war of 1545 and only part of the walls are still standing. Roxburgh Castle has vanished, though the castle mound remains, all that is left after English cannon pounded the stronghold in 1460.

A great deal of Kelso belongs to the Duke of Roxburghe including Floors Castle, which stands outside the town, and the Sunlaws House Hotel, which lies just to the south on the road to Jedburgh. Sunlaws House is a large baronial-style building, popular with shooting and fishing parties, with its own salmon water, a shooting school, 200 acres of park, and good food and accommodation inside when the day's activities are over.

Kelso is a flourishing place. The town square, said to be the largest in Scotland, is surrounded by streets where names like Horsemarket, Cornmarket and Woodmarket give an indication of the trades carried on there. There is a Town Trail which leads the visitor around all the main sights, and some good walks along the banks of the Tweed, from where there are splendid views to Floors Castle.

Floors Castle is extremely grand. It was built in 1721 by the architect William Adam and remodelled about a hundred years later when much of the decorative stonework was added to an already impressive facade. The Duke of Roxburghe still lives there, but house and garden are open to visitors for much of the year.

Treasures include some items of French furniture from the 17th and 18th centuries, a collection of stuffed birds - a popular feature of the Victorian country house - Chinese and Dresden porcelain, and many tapestries and paintings. The park overlooks the Tweed and its small tributary, the Teviot, but the best view hereabouts is of Floors Castle itself, framed between woodlands and looking out to the river below.

Piper, Floors Castle

Twelve miles further west, up the Tweed valley, lies the town and abbey of Melrose. The abbey was built by the King David who founded Kelso Abbey and was destroyed four centuries later by the Earl of Hertford, who demolished

Kelso in the same year. Between those dates Melrose was famous because it held, and may still hold, the heart of King Robert the Bruce, victor of Bannockburn in 1314, which was buried in the abbey. The ruins of Melrose Abbey are very evocative and repay inspection; don't miss the carved figures on the edge of the roof, especially the pig playing the bagpipes.

Next to the abbey is Priorwood Garden, now owned by the National Trust for Scotland, which is set behind high walls and specialises in foliage and plants for dried flower arrangements, and in growing rare apple varieties.

The outstanding places around Melrose are the Eildon Hills, just outside the town, and Sir Walter Scott's home, Abbotsford, three miles away on the banks of the Tweed. The Eildon Hills are the result of volcanic activity, though a legend has it that they were created by the Devil and that King Arthur and his Knights sleep in a cave somewhere under the hills. There is a trail - the Eildon Walk - leading from the centre of Melrose to the 1,500ft-high (457m) crest of the hills, from where there are sweeping views south to the Cheviots and north to the Lammermuirs.

Abbotsford is a large country house set in formal gardens, and crammed with treasures including a large collection of armour. Sir Walter lived here from 1812 until 1832 and his study is as he left it. His library of 9,000 books is still intact, the kitchens are vast and the whole place has been wonderfully well cared for. The most fascinating feature is the collection of relics, displayed in glass cases and ranging from a lock of Bonnie Prince Charlie's hair to Rob Roy's dirk, plus execution warrants and items from the Court of France.

Sir Walter Scott is buried at Dryburgh Abbey, to the east of Melrose, where the honours are shared with Earl Haig, of the whisky family, but better known as commander of the British Armies during the Great War, and founder of the Poppy Day Appeal. Close to Dryburgh is yet another viewpoint, known locally as Scott's View, with wonderful rolling vistas over the surrounding hills.

Nine miles west of Dryburgh is the town of Selkirk. Unlike most of the other towns round about, Selkirk lies on the River Ettrick; it is though another centre for the woollen trade. Sir Walter Scott was the Sheriff or Magistrate of Selkirk and his courtroom is open to visitors. The museum in Halliwell's House tells the story of the town and the woollen trade, and there are plenty of shops selling goods from the local mills.

South of Selkirk lies Hawick - pronounced 'Hoyik' - the largest of the Border towns and another textile centre. The history of the woollen industry in these parts is told in the Hawick Museum, but take note of the horse statue in the main street, which recalls the recapture of the town flag from the English following the disaster at Flodden in 1513. Hawick is one of the many towns that participate in the Border 'Common Ridings'.

The Common Ridings are a relic of the days when the local horsemen rode the town's boundaries to remind the inhabitants, and any encroaching neighbour, of where the town stood and the liberties they intended to maintain. Most of the towns here still hold a Riding, a legacy of the old days of the Border raiders - or reivers.

Now, as then, the horsemen are led by people with old titles - Standard Bearer, Cornet, Braw Lad and, of course, Reiver. The Common Riding in Hawick dates back at least to 1703. The Ridings are held on different dates during the summer and details can be obtained from the TICs. They are entertaining and colourful events, not to be missed.

On the way back to Kelso the A698 passes through Jedburgh. Jedburgh, too, has a Common Riding dating back to Flodden, and another abbey founded by David I and destroyed by the Earl of Hertford. However the abbey church survived and remained in use until 1875. Jedburgh is a centre for the wool trade, full of shops selling scarves, skirts, kilts and sweaters. It also has a 16th-century mansion where Mary, Queen of Scots stayed in 1566. There is a Town Trail which visits the best parts of this attractive little town.

Nine miles to the north-east of Kelso lies the town of Coldstream. No one can be in Coldstream for more than a minute or two without realising that the town is the birthplace of the Coldstream Guards, for a replica of a guardsman hangs from every other shopfront.

The regiment was founded in 1650 from elements of Cromwell's New Model Army and known as Colonel Monck's Regiment of Foot. On 1 January 1660 Colonel Monck marched his regiment to London where they ensured the restoration of King Charles II. Colonel Monck became the first Duke of Albemarle and his regiment the Coldsteam Guards, the only regiment which can trace its origins back to the English Civil War. The Colonel-in-Chief of the Coldstream is HM The Queen, and the Coldstream Museum in the town is well worth a visit.

There is no time perhaps on this weekend for pretty villages like Ford and Etal or the site of Flodden Field near Branxton, 14 miles from Kelso. All that and a lot more must be left for another weekend break on the Scottish Border.

INFORMATION:

KELSO LIES ON THE A698 BETWEEN COLDSTREAM AND HAWICK, AT THE JUNCTION WITH THE A699 FROM SELKIRK.

SUNLAWS HOUSE HOTEL, KELSO, TEL. 0573 450331; EDNAM HOUSE HOTEL, KELSO, TEL. 0573 224168. TIC (KELSO), TEL. 0573 223464; TIC (JEDBURGH), TEL. 0835 863435/863688.

20

Kilfinan and the Cowal Peninsula

—

If the Cowal Peninsula were better known it would attract more visitors and lose some of its elusive charm. That it is little known is surprising for the Cowal Peninsula is not remote, nor hard to get to. It begins at Dunoon, that popular resort on the Firth of Clyde close to Glasgow, running north from there beside Loch Fyne to the town of Inveraray.

This Highland area sandwiched between Loch Fyne and Loch Eck, with Inveraray to the north and the Kyles of Bute to the south, is a peaceful and very beautiful place, perfect for a quiet weekend.

Kilfinan is 75 miles from Glasgow, and 125 miles from Edinburgh.

The Cowal Peninsula is walking or car touring country. There are no really famous sites, and those places there are, while interesting, will not take up much time. The scenery is the great attraction and the routes and roads suggested here are ways to find the best of it.

Every touring area requires a base and the Cowal is well provided with good small hotels. My particular choice is the Kilfinan Hotel at Kilfinan, on the east shore of Loch Fyne, just north of the yachting port at Tighnabruaich. There has been a hotel here since the early years of the 18th century when the Highlands were very wild indeed, but the present establishment is cosy and comfortable and serves excellent food. There are good walks along Loch Fyne and a warm welcome and log fires in the bar when you get back. Who could ask for more?

The Cowal is just one of many peninsulas in this drooping western part of Scotland, but there are a number of ferries which make travel across the lochs easier than it used to be, though their sailings are sometimes erratic and usually summer only. Be aware that there is no ferry at Otter Ferry, a little to the north of Kilfinan, only the old pier. Nor have I seen any otters there; the name comes from the Gaelic *oitir* or 'gravel bank'...and then the Sassenachs got hold of it.

The best way to tour the Cowal is slowly and on minor roads. Begin with a drive north from Kilfinan, after a stroll to the church of St Finian just up the road. The prefix 'Kil' is Gaelic for church and this one is centuries old. Take the road from here towards Strachur, with a stop at the castle at Lachlan.

Castle Lachlan is very photogenic, on a rocky promontory jutting into Loch Fyne, a spot which offers wonderful views towards the coast and hills of Argyll. Some miles up the road lies the village of Strachur, famous today for The Creggans Inn, a very popular hotel and restaurant owned by author, soldier and diplomat Sir Fitzroy Maclean, author of *Eastern Approaches* and numerous works on Scottish history.

Press on north from here, past Hell's Glen and round the top of Loch Fyne to Inveraray. Inveraray Castle, which is situated on the outskirts of this grey, steel-bright little town, is the seat of the Duke of Argyll, Chief of Clan Campbell. This is a fine, turreted example of the style known either as Highland Gothic or Scottish Baronial. The castle is the last of a long line of forts and castles built here by the Campbells to subdue the Macdonalds, who lived in the hills to the north.

Inveraray, though small, is the largest town on the road to the Western Highlands and the ancient capital of Argyll, with a charter dating back to 1474. In those days the town surrounded the castle, but at the end of the 18th century the 3rd Duke decided to build a new home in the park just north of the town, and a new town while he was at it.

The castle is full of treasures, furniture, paintings, weapons, and is well worth a stop; and the town is a fine example of an 18th-century burgh. There is a new tourist attraction in the former gaol or tolbooth. This was the town's prison in the last century and now contains the engagingly named 'Torture, Death and Damnation Exhibition'; audio-recordings of 19th-century murder trials can be heard in the reconstructed 1820 courtroom. There is also the chance to make a fishing net, one of the tasks formerly inflicted on the inmates.

Inveraray has other attractions, including a fish farm and fish-farm teas, and a wildlife park, two miles to the south, with red deer, sika deer, arctic and silver foxes on show. The bell tower in All Saints' church contains the finest set of church bells in Scotland and the second heaviest 'Ring of 10' in the world. There is an easy climb to the top of the tower to see the bells and the stunning views over the countryside.

Inveraray Castle

After seeing Inveraray there is a choice of routes, including the road north across Argyll to Loch Awe and Kilchurn Castle, that most romantic of Highland ruins. However, no one should visit this part of the Highlands without taking the Rest and be thankful Pass road, the A83, through Glen Croe to Tarbet on the shores of Loch Lomond, that splendid lake of song and story.

Just outside Inveraray the road passes the Loch Fyne oyster farm where oysters are bred, smoked and sold. Dunderave Castle was once the stronghold of the chief of Clan MacNaughton, but it is now a family home set on one of those many rocky promontories that jut out into the lake.

The road through the Rest and be thankful Pass is one of the great scenic routes through the Highlands. It winds up to the 2,000ft (609m) mark with the heights of Beinn Ime and Ben Vorlich rearing up to the north, and plenty of footpaths lead from the pass into the surrounding hills.

There is scope for walking, climbing and pony-trekking from all the villages around, as well as sailing and windsurfing on the lochs; but I would urge anyone setting out into the hills to take all the sensible precautions, letting someone know where you are going and when you will be back, wearing the right gear and taking a map and compass.

The A83 was one of the military roads built after the Bonnie Prince Charles rising of 1745, to get cannon into the Highlands and subdue the clans. After the pass comes The Cobbler, another spectacular spot, and then the road falls away to Tarbet and Loch Lomond.

Loch Lomond is glorious but it is not the Cowal; so back to the Rest and be thankful Pass again, and from the pass take the B828 round the smooth side of Ben Donich to Hell's Glen, and back to Strachur. From Strachur it is another delightful run beside Loch Eck to Dunoon, the capital of the Cowal, past one or two interesting places on the way, including Holy Loch, once a base for the American nuclear submarine fleet. Loch Eck is said to be one of the most beautiful of all Scotland's lochs and the road is well provided with lay-bys, parking places and picnic sites.

This country was the home of the great Scottish entertainer, Sir Harry Lauder, who suffered a personal tragedy when his son John was killed in the Great War; Sir Harry erected a memorial to his son which can be seen beside the A815 at the northern end of Loch Eck. Further south, at Benmore, are the Younger Botanic Gardens, which are quite splendid and contain a fine collection of tall Californian redwoods.

Kilmun church is the burial place for the Dukes of Argyll, and then comes Dunoon, a rather smart little resort and a great spot for Glaswegians on a day out. The way of getting from the city to Dunoon was 'Doon the Watter' on one of the old Clyde paddle-steamers, but today most people get to Dunoon by car ferry from Gourock, though there are still steamers on the Clyde and sailing times can be obtained from the TIC in Dunoon.

Dunoon has a golf course and a swimming pool and all the expected resort facilities, and after a look there, another minor road, the B836, leads back over the hills from Sandbank to Ardtaraig and Glendaruel. Take the road over the hill from Glendaruel to Otter Ferry because from the hilltop on a clear day there are amazing views out to the islands of Mull and Jura; this is a superb spot in the evening when the sun is setting in the west.

The Cowal should not be rushed; that is not the way they do things in the Highlands. If all this ground has been covered, there is still the sailing resort of Tighnabruaich and the crossing to the Mull of Kintyre, for views across the sea to the Antrim coast of Northern Ireland. However, I fancy there will be more than enough in the Cowal to keep most people happy for a weekend...or maybe two.

INFORMATION:

KILFINAN LIES BESIDE LOCH FYNE ON THE B8000 BETWEEN STRACHUR AND MILLHOUSE, ON THE WESTERN SIDE OF THE PENINSULA.

THE KILFINAN HOTEL, KILFINAN, TEL. 070 082 201; THE CREGGANS INN, STRACHUR, TEL. 036 986 279. TIC (DUNOON), TEL. 0369 3785; SCOTTISH TOURIST BOARD, TEL. 031 332 2433.

21

Lavenham and the Suffolk Wool Towns

—

The wool towns of England are always worth a visit. They were built in the High Middle Ages, when the creation of splendid buildings was linked to a desire by the wool merchants for some enduring memorial.

The small town of Lavenham is one of the gems of England, beautifully preserved in all its largely medieval glory. It is very popular in summer, so this is a place to visit in spring or autumn when there are fewer people about.

Lavenham is 75 miles from London, and 140 miles from Birmingham.

Lavenham is like nowhere else in England, a town of medieval half-timbered houses leaning drunkenly this way and that, desperately picturesque and full of charm. In its way, Lavenham is not unlike Venice, in the sense that no one would dream of building somewhere like this today; but as with Venice, Lavenham was built when people had no difficulty combining beauty with utility.

In the 15th century this was a wool town, or to be exact a cloth town, for by the middle of the century the wool merchants of England were starting to export the finished cloth. Many of these houses were built to accommodate Flemish wool workers who came to live in the town in the 1450s and teach the local people their skills.

The profits of the wool trade built the church of St Peter and St Paul, one of the finest late Perpendicular-style churches in England, as well as the Guildhall and most of the houses. These profits endowed Lavenham with the wealth of fine buildings which endure to this day.

The best way to see Lavenham is on a walking tour, with the base for a weekend stay The Swan Hotel, one of the most famous medieval inns in England, dating from the mid-15th century.

Lavenham requires explanation as well as exploration and visitors can see the town sites either on a tour with a local guide or by following the route suggested in *A Walk around Lavenham*, a booklet sold by the Tourist Information Centre, which is full of tales about places along the way.

In the early years of the 16th century Lavenham was the fourteenth wealthiest town in England, so there is a lot to see. The best place to begin is in the market place by the Guildhall, which also dates from the first decade of the 16th century and has served as the town hall, the gaol, and now as a museum.

Take a look at the Town Cross, donated by a wool merchant, William Jacob, in 1502, and have a drink at The Angel, one of a number of good inns within the town. The Great House in the corner of the market place is one of several local restaurants. Many of the Lavenham shops are open on Sundays and The Book and Kettle bookshop across the square from The Angel is a source of local material on Lavenham and its surroundings.

Opposite The Greyhound pub in the High Street is the Crooked House, which leans at a most unsteady angle; but one place that should not be missed is the church of St Peter and St Paul. This imposing edifice is on a site which has supported a church since Norman times. The church was rebuilt in the 15th century and although the

Crooked House, Lavenham

Puritans sacked the building in the Civil War, they were unable to destroy all it contains.

Lady Street has some very impressive Tudor half-timbered houses, while Church Street has a fine Georgian house, The Willows, facing up Water Street. A number of local houses, especially the thatched ones, are covered with a pale pink plaster-wash. John Constable, the artist, began his education at the Grammar School in Barn Street, but one of the most interesting houses in the town is The Priory in Water Street, a medieval building which has been lovingly restored and has a herb garden with over 100 different varieties. There is also a café serving lunches, home made cakes and Suffolk cream teas. The Priory was once the home of a community of Benedictine monks and dates from about 1450.

It would be perfectly possible to while away an entire weekend in Lavenham but there are other places nearby which are worth a visit, starting with the small town of Long Melford.

The best way to Long Melford is on the four-mile footpath from Lavenham, along the old railway track and farm trails. This is one of several good walks in the area, which include the three-mile Valley Walk from Rodbridge to Sudbury, and the Melford Walk, a one-mile stroll which takes a circular path around Long Melford. The Tourist Information Centre will provide an illustrated leaflet on all the main walks.

Long Melford gets its name from the High Street that runs for a mile or more through the town, past the antique shops, pubs and cafés and The Bull Hotel, another old hostelry ideal for people exploring these Suffolk wool towns. The Bull was built in 1450 by a wool merchant as his house and trading centre. The house was an inn by 1580 and later a popular staging post for coach travellers on the London road.

Long Melford is not as picturesque as Lavenham and as a result suffers less from summertime crowds. Halfway down the High Street lies Ringers Yard, which supports a number of antique shops. Opposite, and well worth a browse, is My House, a shop selling the less conventional kind of household decoration, like carved and painted life-sized roosters and a selection of wooden piglets.

Other local sights include the huge Church of the Holy Trinity, which has some magnificent 15th-century stained glass, and Melford Hall, a mid-16th-century red-brick house built by an Elizabethan lawyer, Sir William Cordell, Master of the Rolls to Queen Elizabeth I.

Melford Hall is probably the finest example of an Elizabethan house in Suffolk, with splendid gardens and an octagonal Tudor brick pavilion. Inside there is an 18th-century drawing room, a Regency library and a Victorian bedroom. The house is still lived in by the Hyde Parker family who have owned Melford Hall since 1786.

The final place to see on this short visit to Suffolk is the market town of Sudbury. Sudbury is best known as the birthplace of the artist Thomas Gainsborough, who was born here in 1727 in a house in what is now Gainsborough Street. He is commemorated by a statue in the town square and his birthplace is a museum with an exhibition gallery.

Sudbury is the market town for the surrounding villages, dating back to Saxon times. Once a wool town it is now known for silk weaving - the silk for the wedding dress of the Princess of Wales was woven in the town's workshops. Like Lavenham and Long Melford, Sudbury has several interesting medieval buildings, and some well-preserved 18th-century houses in the streets below Market Hill. Larger than the other towns, it has more in the way of shops and entertainment.

INFORMATION:
LAVENHAM LIES ON THE A1141 BETWEEN BURY ST EDMUNDS AND HADLEIGH.

THE SWAN HOTEL, LAVENHAM, TEL. 0787 247477; THE BULL, LONG MELFORD,
TEL. 0787 78494. TIC (LAVENHAM), TEL. 0787 248207; TIC (HADLEIGH), TEL. 0473 822922.

Leominster and the Welsh Marches

—

The Marches can be approached from the north via Shrewsbury, from the south via Gloucester and Cheltenham, or from the east via the M42 and Kidderminster, over Clee Hill.

This is a place for lovers of history, fine country architecture, walking, fishing and pony-trekking, with plenty of scope for people who simply want to amble around pretty towns like Leominster.

Leominster - pronounced 'Lemster' - is 50 miles from Birmingham, 65 miles from Bristol, 70 miles from Cardiff, and 140 miles from London.

The Marches roll plumply towards the mountains of Powys. It looks untroubled nowadays, but for a thousand or so years it was fought over time and again. Norman and Welsh, Yorkist and Lancastrian, Roundhead and Cavalier, all spilt their blood in these parts, but fortunately they left a remarkable amount of the buildings unscathed and villages and towns of venerable beauty and dignity lie round most corners for your delectation and delight.

Three miles north-west of Leominster is the tiny village of Eyton, notable for its church and two fine old houses. One of these, The Marsh, is a 14th-century timbered house restored with care and turned into a country house hotel, one with style and fine food. The proprietors are experts on the area and produce their own guides with suggestions for drives, visits and walks during the weekend.

The Marsh and its gardens lie close to the River Lugg, and an evening stroll to the Old Chain Bridge may bring a sighting of the resident owls or the kingfishers which often visit the stream surrounding the hotel. Leominster lies close by and warrants a gentle walk through its old centre. There are plenty of car parks, but Friday is market day and if you have started the weekend early don't even try to park in Corn Square. Find time to visit the Priory Church, originally part of the 11th-century monastery, School Lane and Corn Square, with their mix of medieval and Tudor buildings. There are over a dozen antique shops to browse in for Leominster is a local centre for the antiques trade.

To the south-west lie the 'black and white' villages with their distinctive half-timbered architecture. These are all medieval villages where the black painting on the timber frames of the houses is set off by the whitewashed wattle-and-daub infilling of the walls, to create a distinctive style.

From Leominster there is a signposted motor-trail that takes you clockwise in a circle of about 40 miles through these villages, to Dilwyn, Weobley, Pembridge and Eardisland on the River Arrow. All these places contain plenty of fine and very photogenic black-and-white buildings, but each has a unique beauty of its own, and most have a good pub for lunch.

Pembridge is typical and worthy of exploration. It was granted a charter for a market by Henry III in 1240 and the Tudor market hall still stands behind the old New Inn, built in 1311 and recommended for its food even now. Round the corner stands a fine church with a peculiar detached bell tower that looks as if it has been transported from Scandanavia, but there are seven similar towers in Herefordshire. A 10p coin in the slot will illuminate the complex workings of the bells, which are all in immaculate order.

Carry on up the road past the Market Hall for a mile and you will reach Dunkertons Cider Co, where you can taste various ciders in a half-timbered off-licence. This is great cider country, though drivers should know that this apple drink can be strong. If you are tempted by Foxwhelp and Strawberry Norman, make sure that you go on Saturday, for Sunday at Dunkertons is a day of rest.

Shobdon lies to the north and has another curious church in a totally different style from that of Pembridge. Around 1750, Richard Bateman, owner of the nearby Shobdon Court, rebuilt the church and decorated it in 'Rococo Gothic' style, similar to Strawberry Hill, Horace Walpole's house

Bell tower, Pembridge

at Twickenham. Everything is painted white and edged in pale blue.

From Shobdon it is a short journey down the B4362 into Wales and the little town of Presteigne. Here the countryside begins to change, the hills become steeper and the forests darker, but Presteigne has kept its 18th-century feel and has the welcoming Radnorshire Arms, a hotel since 1792, although built at the time of the Tudors.

From Presteigne one is spoilt for choice, Knighton or Kington? - not to be confused. Knighton lies to the north and is a good place to tackle part of the Offa's Dyke long-distance footpath as it passes through the town to cross the River Teme. Travel back to Presteigne by the un-classified road that lies to the east of the B4355, called Stonewall Hill. The Anglo-Welsh border runs along this hill and you get magnificent views from here in all directions. Kington, to the south, is another old and delightful town to be explored and savoured, but with so much to see hereabouts, it may be wise to devote the weekend to a theme, perhaps on gardens or stately homes.

In practice these themes can be combined. For gardens, one could begin with the one back at The Marsh, which won the Hotel Garden of the Year Award in 1991. If you can tear yourself away from the lily pond and the flower-bordered croquet lawn, there are 12 major gardens and nurseries within easy reach, including four containing National Collections.

Abbey Dore Court houses the sedum and euphorbia collection; Burford House, near Tenbury Wells, is in charge of clematis; Hergest Croft in Kington has responsibility for maples and birches; and The Picton Garden at Colwall holds Michaelmas daisies. Each and every garden varies in its appeal as the seasons go by, so you can pick and choose from others such as Broadfield Court at Bodenham and Dinmore Manor south of Leominster. Just mark them up on a map and tour around, whenever possible on minor roads.

You don't really need to drive that far for good stately homes. Berrington Hall is on Leominster's northern doorstep and stands in a park laid out by Capability Brown. The house was built by Henry Holland in 1778 for Thomas Harley, who made his fortune supplying clothing for the British Army in America and used his wealth to decorate his house in the neo-classical fashion. Most of the house is open for viewing, including the Victorian laundry, the Georgian dairy and the servants' hall, now a tearoom.

Four miles to the north-west lies Croft Castle, which dates back to the 14th century and has 18th-century additions and a fine collection of Georgian chairs. One of the Croft ancestors was tutor to the young Prince Edward, later Edward IV, and his brother Richard, later Richard III.

The Croft Castle park is open all year round and is a good place for a walk. Waymarked paths will take you from the car park to Croft Ambrey Iron Age hill-fort, which is an extraordinary viewpoint. Choose a clear day and you can apparently see 14 counties. How you recognise them all is a different matter.

On Sundays and Bank Holidays the 18th-century watermill at Mortimer's Cross opens its doors and those of a mechanical mind can explore its workings. Those less interested in such things can visit the upper rooms which house a small museum devoted to the 1461 battle of Mortimer's Cross beside the River Lugg, one of the decisive battles in the Wars of the Roses, won by Edward IV. A collection of rare breeds of animals and birds also inhabits the site.

A few miles to the north of here lies Ludlow, with all it has to offer; castle and river, old streets and houses, market and coffee shops, all luring you to browse around contentedly for hours. But be warned, if you cram Ludlow into your weekend as well as everything else, you will need a break to get over it all.

INFORMATION:

LEOMINSTER LIES AT THE JUNCTION OF THE A49 FROM HEREFORD TO LUDLOW WITH THE A44 FROM WORCESTER TO KINGTON.

THE MARSH COUNTRY HOTEL, EYTON, TEL. 0568 613952; THE RADNORSHIRE ARMS, PRESTEIGNE, TEL. 0544 267406. TIC (LEOMINSTER), TEL. 0568 616460; TIC (LUDLOW), TEL. 0584 875053.

23

Lincoln

—

The city of Lincoln is dominated by the great cathedral that has stood on the hill here since 1280, a magnificent building which can be seen for miles across the surrounding countryside. With such a splendid centrepiece Lincoln could hardly fail to provide a great many attractions for a weekend break. The local guide book offers '101 Things to See and Do' and that may be an underestimate, so what follows can only be a selection.

Lincoln is a popular spot for summer tourists and therefore best visited in the spring or autumn. Springtime is especially good because the bulb fields to the east are in full flower.

Lincoln is 70 miles from Leeds, 85 miles from Manchester, 90 miles from Birmingham, and 140 miles from London.

Lincoln is a very old town. The countryside around is flat, and whoever held Lincoln hill held sway over the entire area. That thought certainly occurred to the Romans who built a fort here in AD48, and around that stronghold grew the fortress city of Lindum. From here the Romans could guard two great roads, the Fosse Way and Ermine Street, which can still be followed across the countryside.

The settlement expanded and became a colony, and in time Lincoln - or Lindum - became one of the finest Roman cities in Britain. It had a forum and colonnaded streets, an aqueduct and an underground sewerage system that was unique at the time. The Romans also began to drain the surrounding lands and some of the canals they cut are in use to this day.

Lincoln still has a sizeable number of Roman remains. Parts of the old forum still exist by the cathedral, together with a Roman well and

Newport Arch, which straddles the northern exit from the city and is the oldest archway still used by traffic. A recent addition, installed by the citizens, is a Roman herb garden on the site of the St Paul-in-the-Bail church. The church was pulled down in 1971 and excavations on the site revealed a series of churches and burial places going back to Roman times.

All the herbs on display in the garden were introduced to this country by the Romans. They include chives, which were used for kidney problems; clary sage, which helped relieve inflammation and infection of the eyes; Lemon Balm, to flavour fish; marjoram, which is efficacious in the treatment of headaches; and many more. Wandering around the Herb Garden is a pleasant way to spend an evening.

The Romans left at the end of the 5th century and the Anglo-Saxons, who followed them, used the site of Lincoln as a quarry for dressed stone. Then came the Danes, who established a thriving town. By the 11th century this Danish settlement was reduced to a small village full of peasant farmers, who were evicted in 1067 when William the Conqueror passed this way.

William was a military man and the location of Lincoln just ached for a castle. He began to erect both the present fortress and the cathedral, which was started in 1072 and took another 200 years to complete.

The town of Lincoln took root on the hilltop, around the cathedral and the castle. Wise visitors will spend most of their time up on the hill, for the town below has not been improved by late 20th-century developments. Far better to drive up to the White Hart Hotel in Bailgate, and start from there.

The White Hart is close to all the historic sites and in the very centre of the old town. Parts of the hotel date back to 1387 when Richard II was a guest, and the hotel dining room is named King Richard's Restaurant and decorated with portraits from the later days of Plantagenet rule.

The hotel is worth a closer look for it has played a part in the history of Lincoln. The plans for the first armoured tank were thought up in a room at the White Hart in September 1915; 200 tanks were subsequently built in the town and used at the Battle of Flers, on the Somme, a year later. The hotel bars also entertained many of the RAF and USAAF airmen from the bomber bases nearby during the Second World War, and these men too are commemorated within the hotel. The drawing room contains a large collection of clocks.

Having settled in at the White Hart, the next step will be a visit to the castle or the cathedral. The castle is in excellent preservation and there is a good stroll round the battlements from where there are spectacular views across the city and to the tower of Boston Stump, miles away across the Lincolnshire landscape. The castle has two mottes or mounds, and was used in the last century as a prison, a period recalled in an exhibition in the former prison chapel.

Lincoln Cathedral is certainly worth a couple of visits over the weekend. One visit might begin with a walk round the outer walls and under the flying buttresses which support the nave and chancel, for the outside of the cathedral is quite magnificent. The Bishop of Lincoln once presided over the largest bishopric in England, which ran from the Humber to the Thames, and the cathedral reflects such power and influence.

Lincoln Cathedral has had its ups and downs. A fire destroyed much of the fabric in 1141 and an earthquake shattered the rest in 1185, so that the original Norman structure had to be rebuilt by Bishop Hugh of Avalon, the work beginning in 1186 and taking the best part of 100 years to complete.

Bishop (later St) Hugh also began the Bishop's Palace which housed the diocese until the Reformation. The palace then fell into decay and finally collapsed in the mid-17th century. Enough remains to give an idea of the original building, and the grounds contain a vineyard, thought to be the most northerly in Europe, the vines protected from the north winds by the bulk of the cathedral.

Lincoln Cathedral is built on the grand scale. The tower is 271ft (83m) high and houses the Great Tom bell which strikes the hours for the city. There are two rose windows dating from 1225 and the small gargoyle known as the 'Lincoln Imp', as well as a splendid treasury and the chapels of the Lincolnshire Regiment and Bomber Command. The Bomber Command chapel contains memorial windows and a Remembrance Book listing the names of 26,000 airmen who flew from Lincolnshire during the last war and failed to return.

The best way down into the rest of the city from the cathedral is via Steep Hill, which falls away sharply on a cobbled pathway. This street contains Jew's House and the adjacent Jew's Court, which date from the 12th century. Jew's House is one of the finest early medieval houses in Britain. Lincoln once supported a thriving Jewish community until the Jews were driven out of England in 1290 after a series of massacres. Steep Hill has a number of shops and restaurants and smart boutiques, as well as the Wig and Mitre, a 14th-century pub, and leads down to Michaelgate and Christ's Hospital Terrace, and the lower town.

Modern Lincoln contains many Tudor elements and another medieval relic, High Bridge, which dates back to Norman times and is the oldest bridge in England to carry buildings, rather like the Ponte Vecchio in Florence. The buildings date from the 16th century.

National Cycle Museum

Near here lies Brayford Pool, now a canal boat station but once a thriving shipping point for the local trade in grain and garden produce. At one time

Lincoln was the fourth largest port in England, though it lies 40 miles from the sea.

Other sights to see include the Museum of Lincolnshire Life in the old militia barracks, which is a very fine example of a local history museum, and the Usher Art Gallery, which was built and endowed by a local businessman, James Usher, to house his extensive collection of watches, clocks and porcelain. There is also the National Cycle Museum at Brayford Wharf.

The River Witham provides one of the city's more light-hearted entertainments, an evening river cruise complete with music and disco dancing; or, during summer days, there are one-hour cruises on the Fossdyke canal. There is good shopping at the Freshney Place shopping mall on the road to Grimsby, where visitors can be entertained with jugglers, music, restaurants and live theatre, and there is more theatre and films on offer at the Ritz Theatre in Lincoln High Street.

Five miles west of the city lies Doddington Hall, built in 1600 and one of the most beautiful Elizabethan mansions in the country. It has a Tudor gatehouse, splendid walled gardens, a grass maze, a temple of the winds and a nature trail.

Doddington Hall is well worth a visit, but most of this Lincoln weekend will be spent in the old city, around the great cathedral on the hill.

INFORMATION:

LINCOLN LIES ON THE A46 BETWEEN NEWARK AND MARKET RASEN.

THE WHITE HART HOTEL, LINCOLN, TEL. 0522 526222; GARDEN COURT HOTEL, LINCOLN,
TEL. 0522 544244. TIC (LINCOLN), TEL. 0522 529828.

24

Matlock and the White Peak

—

The Peak District of Derbyshire and Staffordshire is so beautiful and so strategically sited that it deserves to be the setting for two of the weekends in this book. This weekend concentrates on the south of the District, in the limestone 'White Peak' around the towns of Matlock and Matlock Bath. The area lies within the confines of the Peak District National Park and offers a great variety of things to see and do, both in the towns and the country-side round about.

Matlock is 45 miles from Manchester, 60 miles from Birmingham, 65 miles from Leeds, and 150 miles from London.

The White Peak lies in the southern parts of the Peak District, below the town of Matlock. The countryside of the White Peak differs from that of the High or 'Dark' Peak in having fewer open moors and more dales, plus some delightful river valleys - of which two, Dovedale and the Manifold Valley, are splendid for walking.

The other feature of this part of the Peak District is the limestone crags or 'tors', a word more familiar to Dartmoor but used up here in the same sense of a lone jutting outcrop. High Tor near Matlock Bath and Chee Tor in the valley of the River Wye are two good examples. Both are very popular with climbers.

The area is seamed with dales, sheltered spots where birds and wildflowers flourish, and criss-crossed with stone walls and winding footpaths, quite delightful to explore. There is sailing available on Carsington Reservoir and some of the hotels offer guests the chance to fish on the local rivers.

As a base for a weekend in this southern part of Derbyshire there is the Riber Hall Hotel, just outside the town of Matlock and close to the gaunt ruins of Riber Castle and the Riber Wildlife Park.

Riber Hall is partly Elizabethan, and noted hereabouts for the quality of its food and wine list. The hotel is open all year round, and serves lunch or dinner to non-residents. The gardens at Riber Hall are wild and beautiful; and the view across the valley is especially fine and runs up to the escarpment, which appears to be crowned by a lighthouse. This is a memorial to the Sherwood Foresters Regiment set above Crich, a memorial which is illuminated on the anniversary of any Great War battle in which the Sherwood Foresters took part.

Like Buxton further north, Matlock and Matlock Bath used to be spa towns. They are now resorts and centres for touring the area, which means they can be crowded in summer when people leave their cars to walk beside the River Derwent or take the cable car up to the Heights of Abraham, set on the summit of a 60-acre country park. Here, among a variety of other attractions, are guided tours through some of the underground caverns.

The Heights of Abraham is strictly for tourists. Other visitors might prefer one of the other local attractions like the National Tramway Museum at Crich, south-east of Matlock, which is both interesting and great fun.

The museum has been open for more than 30 years and has assembled a great assortment of vehicles, featuring the various stages of development of the tramway age. There are electric trams and horse-drawn trams and trams which run on tracks, some displayed in the depots, some still running on track laid through the grounds, giving passengers spectacular views of the Derwent Valley. Even people who don't normally care for museums - or trams - might find a visit here enjoyable.

The Peak District was once a lead-mining area and still supports a number of quarries. The 200-year-old history of the Derbyshire lead miners is displayed in the Peak Mining Museum in Matlock Bath.

The Peak District can also boast three stately homes. The most notable is probably Chatsworth, the home of the 11th Duke of

Devonshire, who inspite of his title, is an important landowner in Derbyshire and very popular with the local people.

The Cavendish family has lived at Chatsworth for the last 450 years, ever since Bess of Hardwick built the original house here in 1555, before going on to build Hardwick Hall nearby. The Elizabethan building was rebuilt at the end of the 17th century by Bess's great-great-grandson, the 1st Duke of Devonshire, and each generation since has done something to improve the fabric or the park which surrounds it; including, inevitably, hiring the talents of Capability Brown.

The good thing about a visit to Chatsworth is that the tours are not guided. Visitors follow a marked route and can spend as much time as they like looking at the various treasures, tapestries, paintings, furniture or porcelain. The gardens cover more than 100 acres and contain the famous Cascade, a number of jets, fountains and waterfalls, a rose garden and a tropical greenhouse. Half a day would hardly be enough to see even a part of it, but once Chatsworth has been examined there is still Haddon Hall, a magnificent medieval pile a mile south of Bakewell, where many of the furnishings date back to the 14th and 15th centuries.

The White Peak though is first and foremost an outdoor area, which can only be fully appreciated by leaving the car from time to time to go walking or cycling.

To visit just some of the places, take the A5012 west from Matlock Bath and pick up the A515 and B5054 for the village of Hartington. Hartington is a good walking centre and noted for the manufacture of Stilton cheese which, with many other English cheeses, can be purchased from a small shop by the village green. There is also a good pub, the Devonshire Arms, and the Charles Cotton Hotel. This is named after Charles Cotton the poet, who became more famous as a fisherman. Cotton was born in 1630 and became a friend of Izaak Walton, with whom he used to go fishing on the River Dove nearby. In 1676 Cotton contributed a section to Walton's classic book, *The Compleat Angler*, which actually begins with describing the fishing at Hartington.

The border with Staffordshire begins just south of Hartington, which is a good place to start a walk down Dovedale. Dovedale is a seven-mile-long, rocky valley, running south from Hartington to Thorpe, with a clear trail that runs under the beech and nut trees and beside or over the rushing River Dove.

Both Dovedale and the equally attractive Manifold Valley can be reached from the village of Thorpe. Here a hotel called Peveril of the Peak is a good choice for walkers. The hotel sits at the foot of the 900ft-high (274m) Thorpe Cloud hill, and good footpaths begin at the hotel car park. The hotel began as Thorpe rectory and the views from the Peakstone Restaurant are superb, especially in the early evening.

Well-dressing

Close to Thorpe is another beautiful and interesting village, Tissington, which is famous for well-dressing and the main departure point for the Tissington Trail, a walking and mountain-biking route that follows the track of the old railway for 14 miles up to Hartington. Mountain bikes for making this expedition can be hired at Tissington.

Derbyshire well-dressing probably dates back to pagan times but it was revived in Tissington in the early part of the 17th century, during the harshest period of the Puritan domination, and has continued to flourish here ever since. The underlying purpose is to give thanks for the continuous flow of pure spring water, by decorating the wells with large religious pictures made by pressing flower petals into soft mud spread out on wooden frames.

The delicacy and detail achieved by the local people in making these flower pictures cannot be adequately described in words, but since well-dressing goes on throughout the spring and summer, there are plenty of chances to see examples.

If time permits the village of Ilam should be visited before taking a walk through the Manifold Valley. Nearby lies the village of Ellastone, which was the setting for George Eliot's novel, *Adam Bede*, and many other local places such as Wootton, Okeover and Stanton also appear in fictional guise in Eliot's 'Loamshire'.

But the White Peak has no need of fictional embellishment. This ruggedly beautiful part of England is full of countryside delights and perfect for a quiet weekend or two.

INFORMATION:

MATLOCK LIES ON THE A6 BETWEEN DERBY AND BAKEWELL.

RIBER HALL, MATLOCK, TEL. 0629 582795; PEVERIL OF THE PEAK, THORPE, TEL. 033529 333. TIC (MATLOCK), TEL. 0629 55082.

25

Melton Mowbray and the Hunting Shires

—

The Hunting Shires of Leicestershire, Northamptonshire and the former Rutland have much to offer the weekend visitor, quite apart from their central situation.

A visit to the shires can be made at any time of the year, for there is always something to do there. As a starting point for exploring the region, I have chosen the town of Melton Mowbray.

Melton Mowbray is 60 miles from Birmingham, 90 miles from Manchester, 95 miles from Leeds, and 110 miles from London.

Melton Mowbray in Leicestershire is generally accepted as the capital of the Hunting Shires. Even those who abhor hunting and would never take a day out with the Quorn, the Cottesmore or the Belvoir Hunt can still enjoy the splendid scenery of these Midland counties, while roaming through villages with wonderful Old English names like Frisby on the Wreake, Staunton in the Vale, Burton on the Wolds and Barnaby in the Willows.

Take note of these pretty places and the spires of their churches for this is hunting and jumping country, the place where the point-to-point or steeplechasing was first invented. At the turn of the 18th century, when the day's hunt was over, the huntsmen would use up any spare energy in man or horse by 'steeplechasing', a highly dangerous race across country over ditch and wall and fence, galloping in a direct line from one church steeple to the next.

There are a lot of church steeples around Melton Mowbray, but clearly steeplechasing did not always exhaust the participants, for Melton Mowbray has some curious tales to tell of hunting folk and hunting ways.

For example, this is the place that gave rise to the saying about 'painting the town red'. This phrase dates back to 1837 when the then Marquis of Waterford and his chums, somewhat excited and elevated after a day on horseback and an evening on the claret, got some buckets of red paint and spread it all over the town, daubing the town hall and most of the High Street, and a constable who came to restrain them.

Earnest seekers after some sign of this aristocratic vandalism will be disappointed, but there are still a few sights worth seeing in the town centre including the church of St Mary, which dates from 1170 and has a tower more than 100ft (30m) high. Sir Malcolm Sargent, who conducted the Albert Hall Promenade Concerts for many years, used to be the organist at St Mary's.

The Harboro' House Hotel in Burton Street is the place where the hunting folk usually stay. The Anne of Cleves House further up the same street was built in 1384 and belonged for a while to the lady herself, the fourth of Henry VIII's wives. Melton Mowbray is also famous for Stilton cheese and pork pies, both of which can be purchased from The Old Pork Pie Shoppe in Nottingham Street, near the market place.

With all that said, Melton Mowbray itself can be covered adequately in an hour or two on Saturday morning, which is market day in the town. That done, it is time to take a look at some of the surrounding villages and make an excursion to Belvoir Castle and Bosworth Field.

Frisby on the Wreake, five miles west of Melton Mowbray, used to be England's answer to Gretna Green. In the 18th century the parish vicar would marry couples without calling the banns or requiring a licence. The main attraction of the village today is the walks along the Wreake and the nearby canal, and a pub lunch at the Black Horse Inn.

Waltham on the Wolds, six miles north of Melton Mowbray, is rather prettier, and a lot chillier when a north-east wind comes sweeping over the flatlands from the Wash. Waltham is a medieval and Tudor village where many of the houses are four or five hundred years old. Until 1921 the village belonged to the Duke of Rutland, who lived at Belvoir Castle just a few miles to the north. Waltham today is full of racing stables and the streets tend to be crowded with strings of horses making their way to the nearby gallops.

The Vale of Belvoir - pronounced 'Beaver' - is a beautiful stretch of country, a patchwork of fields, woods and copses clearly designed to provide some thrilling gallops and a few stiff fences. Belvoir Castle, which overlooks the Vale, has been the home of the Earls and Dukes of Rutland since the Dissolution of the Monasteries in Henry VIII's reign, though the present house, complete with crenellations, has been considerably altered down the years.

The house contains the anticipated collection of furniture, paintings and tapestries found in well cared for stately homes and, more surprisingly, the museum of that distinguished and gallant regiment, the 17th/21st Lancers. Among their collection of medals, weapons and mess silver is the bugle that sounded the charge at Balaclava.

Memories of an earlier engagement can be found in the great historical attraction of Bosworth Field, which lies near Market Bosworth, 12 miles west of Leicester, about an hour by car from Melton Mowbray and well worth the trip.

The battle of Bosworth Field on 22 August 1485 saw the end of the Plantagenet dynasty and the arrival of the Tudors, and even those who are only marginally interested in history will find a visit here fascinating. The battlefield has hardly changed since 1485 and the events of the day are clearly explained by signboards around the location and in the excellent Visitors' Centre, which has armour and weapons and all manner of exhibits and a small cinema which shows the Bosworth battle scenes from Laurence Olivier's film, *Richard III*. The whole presentation is lightly handled and very well done.

King Richard's standard, Battle of Bosworth

Those who don't care for history but would enjoy a little exercise can walk the battlefield trail that runs for a couple of miles around the countryside. The town of Market Bosworth is just two miles from the battlefield and has several good pubs.

As a centre for touring this region there are a number of hotels and the health hydro at Ragdale Hall, west of Melton Mowbray, where the treatments are not obligatory, the food is good and the bar full of entertaining folk. A two-night stopover entitles the guest to a small number of treatments and those who choose to stay elsewhere can take advantage of one of the Day Guest Packages, which start with a health check and include all manner of exercises and treatments.

Among hotels worthy of consideration is one with hunting connections, the small and friendly Whipper-In Hotel in the market town of Oakham, 10 miles south of Melton Mowbray. The Whipper-In is decorated with English hunting prints and has comfortable rooms and good English food.

Another option is the Hambleton Hall Hotel, which is set on a long peninsula of land, high above the surrounding countryside and jutting out into Rutland Water, the largest man-made lake in Europe. The hotel is part of the Relais-et-Chateaux group and offers a high standard of food and accommodation.

Oakham, formerly the county town of Rutland, is much prettier than the modern Melton Mowbray. Oakham Castle dates from 1191, and the history of Rutland County, which officially vanished 20 years ago but is kept alive by the local people, is fully displayed in the Rutland Museum. All Saints' church went up in the 13th century and Oakham School is one of the oldest in the country, dating back to 1584. Oakham is kept busy today by people attracted to the pleasures on and around Rutland Water.

Exloring Rutland Water could take a full day. The lake has been organised as a leisure centre and the attractions include a Birdwatching Centre at Egleton, a 450-acre nature reserve equipped with hides allowing good views of the waterfowl. Tropical butterflies and the underwater world of Rutland Water are on view at the Butterfly and

Aquatic Centre by Sykes Lane, and cycles can be hired at Whitwell on the lake for a 17-mile ride around the shoreline. This ride extends to 23 miles if the cyclist rides up to Hambleton and has a break at Hambleton Hall. Rutland Water also has fishing, sailing, windsurfing and pleasure cruises, and there is golf available at the Rutland Water Golf Course.

Leicestershire is full of things to see and do, enough for several weekends. The Rutland Railway Museum at Cottesmore has steam trains, and there are fine gardens at Halstead House on the B6047 south of Melton Mowbray.

If the weather is dreary there are two fine towns in easy reach. Nottingham, 18 miles away, has the castle where Robin Hood's old enemy, the Sheriff, used to lurk, as well as the Trip to Jerusalem, a pub which has stood beneath the castle walls since medieval times and was a gathering point for pilgrims setting out for the Holy Land.

Leicester, 16 miles from Melton Mowbray, is better known for its street markets and for the new Shires Centre, the largest shopping mall in the country. It contains department stores and more than 80 shops and boutiques ready to compete with the Leicester Retail Market, which has been in existence for over 700 years and still fields 500 stalls selling everything from fresh fruit to handbags.

Taken together, town and country, rural attractions and Rutland Water, the Hunting Shires have everything needed for an enjoyable weekend break.

INFORMATION:

MELTON MOWBRAY LIES AT THE JUNCTION OF THE A606 FROM OAKHAM TO NOTTINGHAM WITH THE A607 FROM GRANTHAM TO LEICESTER.

RAGDALE HALL, RAGDALE, TEL. 0664 434831; THE WHIPPER-IN HOTEL, OAKHAM, TEL. 0572 756971; HAMBLETON HALL, HAMBLETON, TEL. 0572 756991. TIC (MELTON MOWBRAY), TEL. 0664 69946.

26

Mersea Island and the Constable Country

—

No two places could provide such a contrast as Mersea Island on the north shore of the Blackwater estuary, which is flat and waterlogged and fringed with boats and sailing craft, and the beautiful, rolling Constable Country just to the north of Colchester, on the Essex-Suffolk border. Though very different, both places have their attractions and are linked through the town of Colchester, which is one of the oldest towns in Britain. Considered together they provide all the varied ingredients for a good weekend, especially in the spring and early autumn. Summertime tends to be crowded and winter in Mersea can be less than inviting.

Mersea Island is 70 miles from London.

Mersea is a part-time island. For most of the time a causeway connects it with the mainland across the Pyfleet channel, one of the arms of the River Colne, and puts it within easy reach of Colchester, seven miles to the north; but at some high tides, and especially during the high spring tides, the causeway is covered and the island cut off.

That is when Mersea appears at its best, as an isolated spot, a place apart, sunk in the Essex marshes. For some, Mersea is at its most appealing during the oyster season from October to March, when local oysters are sold from stalls along the hard at West Mersea, and the river mist comes creeping down the Blackwater. At such times, Mersea Island is somewhere straight out of *Great Expectations*.

Apart from the oysters and sailing activities, there is a fine church, topped with a sailing ship weather vane, and during the summer months, the Mersea Island Museum in the High Street of West Mersea, which tells all there is to know of this curious and isolated little island.

Fishing boats, West Mersea

Mersea is a place for sailors and birdwatchers - there is a good bird reserve at Fingringhoe Wick - and for those who enjoy quiet places off the beaten track. Creature comforts are available at the Blackwater Hotel and Restaurant in West Mersea. Originally a Victorian coaching inn, this comfortable little hotel is set right in the centre of West Mersea, close to the beach.

From the Blackwater Hotel the hinterland of Essex is in easy reach through the town of Colchester, a greatly underrated place with much to see and do. This includes Colchester Zoo, which has rare animals like the snow leopard and the Siberian tiger, which the zoo is attempting to conserve. There is an excellent Social History Museum and Hollytrees, a museum devoted to the history of toys; as well as the Natural History Museum, which has lots of those currently popular hands-on attractions and exhibits. These and two other museums - the Castle Museum and Tymperleys Clock Museum - are housed in historic buildings in the town centre.

One of the latest Colchester attractions is Leisure World, which has a pool and water chutes, fitness centres, squash and badminton courts, and embraces Charter Hall, which puts on concerts, plays and exhibitions; as does the nearby Mercury Theatre.

Colchester dates back to Roman times and, now as then, is a garrison town. It has comprehensive shopping along the Red Lion pedestrian precinct and, all in all, is a good place to spend a Saturday morning or to find some entertainment on Saturday night.

The famous 'Constable Country' lies just eight miles to the north of Colchester around Dedham Vale, East Bergholt and along the valley of the River Stour, that placid stream which divides Essex from Suffolk.

Like Mersea Island, the Constable Country is best visited outside the summer months of July and August, and for the same reason - people. The place to start a tour is at Dedham, by common consent the heart of Constable Country, and a very pretty village. From Dedham it is possible to walk down the river bank to Flatford Mill, but you might prefer to hire a boat and row down the Stour to Flatford Mill and Willy Lott's cottage, and so view the scene pictured in Constable's *The Hay Wain*. The old mill at Flatford, now owned by the National Trust, is a Field Study Centre where, naturally enough, painting is one of the subjects on offer.

Dedham village has good pubs and a lot of pink-washed houses, and the grammar school which Constable attended, though this has been transformed into a couple of private houses. Constable was born in East Bergholt, another pretty place with the excellent Red Lion pub and a rather curious church. The church tower was never completed because, or so legend has it, the Devil came along every night and undid the builders' work.

A more likely explanation is that the money ran out, but whatever the reason, the church bells are kept in a low building beside the church, from where they are rung every Sunday by men who can stand among them as they chime. Constable's parents and Willy Lott, who worked for the Constable family, are both buried in the churchyard.

None of the villages in Constable Country are very far apart and most of them can be reached on footpaths as well as on minor roads. A good touring base for this part of the country is the Maison Talbooth, a well-appointed country house hotel looking out over Dedham Vale and matched by Le Talbooth Restaurant, which stands on the banks of the Stour nearby.

Maison Talbooth is set in a Victorian mansion surrounded by parkland, looking down on the medieval village of Stratford St Mary, while Le Talbooth is a half-timbered restaurant, quite old but carefully restored. Those who do not stay at Maison Talbooth should try and fit in lunch or dinner at the restaurant during a visit to the area. The setting by the river is sublime.

One of the pleasures on a visit to Constable Country is to take along a book of his paintings and try and fit them to the present scenes. This is far from easy, for many of the buildings have changed and trees have grown or died, with new ones planted. Some places have survived better than others.

Among these are the village of Stoke-by-Nayland, five miles from Stratford St Mary. The church at Stoke-by-Nayland and the village itself have featured in many of Constable's paintings and it is not hard to see why. This is one of the prettiest villages in the county, full of thatched and colour-washed Tudor cottages, while the church is Perpendicular Gothic with a tower over 100ft (30m) high.

Nayland, a mile down the B1087, is another attractive village, with a very good restaurant, Martha's Vineyard, which is shut on Sundays and serves only dinner. Nayland church contains a famous Constable painting, *Christ Blessing the Bread and Wine*, and there are lots more half-timbered cottages and an entertaining walk down Fen Street, where a series of footbridges lead to and fro across the stream.

This part of Constable Country is less well known and less crowded than the area around Flatford Mill and Dedham, but with plenty of places to see, like the village of Bures and the clapboard mill at Halstead, or the circular church at Little Maplestead. This is a very rare example of this type of church, one modelled on the Holy Sepulchre in Jerusalem and built in the 12th century by the Knights of St John.

Moving back towards the south and Mersea Island, the Beth Chatto Gardens near Colchester should not be missed and some of the places north of the River Blackwater are also worth inspection.

Tolleshunt D'Arcy on the B1026 south-west of Colchester has a fine Elizabethan mansion surrounded by a moat, and there is good walking along the banks of the estuary from Tollesbury to the yachting resort of Maldon.

To call Maldon a 'resort' may be a trifle unfair, for the local sailors take their yachting seriously, as they have to do in these shallow, tidal East Coast waters. A 'sailing centre' might be more appropriate, but even people with no interest in boats will find Maldon enjoyable. Parts of the town date back to the 15th century, the church has a strange triangular tower, and the yacht- and dinghy-thronged waterfront is always a scene of activity.

Heybridge and the Heybridge Basin, just to the east of Maldon, is another great yachting centre, and from there it is a pleasant drive back to Mersea - circling north through Great Braxted, past the bird reserve at Abberton Reservoir, with a short diversion to Chappel on the A604 west of Colchester to visit the East Anglian Railway Museum.

INFORMATION:

MERSEA ISLAND LIES ON THE B1025, SOUTH OF COLCHESTER. EAST BERGHOLT AND DEDHAM LIE JUST EAST OF THE A12 BETWEEN COLCHESTER AND IPSWICH.

THE BLACKWATER HOTEL, WEST MERSEA, TEL. 0206 383338; MAISON TALBOOTH, DEDHAM, TEL. 0206 322367; LE TALBOOTH RESTAURANT, TEL. 0206 323150. TIC (COLCHESTER), TEL. 0206 712920.

27

Muirfield and Lammermuir

—

One of the many pleasures of writing a book like this is that the travelling and research take you to places where you might not otherwise go. Places that are off the regular tourist trails and often turn out to be quite delightful; and so it was on this weekend.

The village of Gullane lies on the southern coast of the Firth of Forth, facing south towards the Lammermuir country, just the spot for a quiet weekend.

Gullane is 20 miles from Edinburgh, 70 miles from Glasgow, and 110 miles from Newcastle.

I have been lucky enough to do a great deal of travelling in my life but few places I have visited are as beautiful or as surprising as the Lammermuir Hills and the country of Berwickshire, south-east of Edinburgh. The beauty lies in the rolling hills and unspoiled coast, the surprise in the fact that somewhere so beautiful should be so little known.

My base here is the village or small town of Gullane on the Firth of Forth, best known for the golf course at Muirfield and the Greywalls hotel nearby. While this part of Scotland may be generally unfamiliar to the world at large, it is a mecca for golfers, as is Greywalls where the champions stay. Every hotel worth visiting should have something special to offer, and Greywalls has excellent golf and fine architecture.

There are 10 first-class golf courses close to Greywalls, including the course at Muirfield. The quality of the golf can be judged from the hotel guest list which boasts such regulars as Arnold Palmer, Nick Faldo, Greg Norman and Lee Trevino, and a score more besides.

The hotel is a former country house, built by Sir Edwin Lutyens at the turn of the century, with gardens created by his collaborator, Gertrude Jekyll. People who do not stay at Greywalls should stop to see the rose garden and the other parts of the grounds, divided from each other by holly hedges.

Coast and countryside are the two attractions of Berwickshire. Both are best seen by walking or car touring. The first tour to make is down the coast to the English border at Berwick-upon-Tweed. There is a Fishing Heritage Trail which can be picked up at Port Seton, to the west of Gullane and close to Prestonpans, site of one of the many 18th-century battles between English Redcoats and Highlanders supporting the Stuarts.

There are many splendid castles on this route. At Tantallon, a fine if much eroded fortress can be observed glaring out across the Firth to the Bass Rock. There is another at Dirleton, dating from the 12th century, and a third at Hailes near East Linton. On the tip of the cape lies the port of North Berwick from where there are trips to the Bass Rock, Scotland's Gibraltar, a place besieged many times over the centuries.

The Bass Rock has a long and varied history. In AD606 it sheltered a hermit, St Baldred. The Lauder family acquired the Rock in 1316 and owned it for 600 years, as a prison, a fortress and a Jacobite stronghold.

Bass Rock

When the Bass Rock surrendered to the Hanovarian forces in 1694, it was the last place in the kingdom to hold out for King James II. Today the island is a bird sanctuary and hosts a huge colony of gannets.

North Berwick is a pleasant town overlooked by a conical hill called 'The Law', which is topped by an arch made from the jawbones of whales. Apart from the gannets and gulls, one of the other flying exhibits along this coast is the Museum of Flight at East Fortune which has a well cared for collection of aircraft, a must for aviation buffs.

The next stop down the coast is Dunbar, a fine town, a popular seaside resort, and the birthplace of John Muir, founder of the American National Park system and the Sierra Club and a man generally regarded as the Father of Conservation, who was born here in 1838.

The bird-haunted John Muir Country Park just to the west of the town is well worth a visit, and this is followed by the road to Cockburnspath from where there is a coastal walk along the cliffs to St Abb's Head, which supports another seabird colony with gulls and gannets and all manner of birds nesting on the cliffs.

Finally, just before the border is the still active fishing port of Eyemouth, which has a good local history museum featuring the story of the town; fishing and farming, boat building and smuggling. There is a fine collection of seabirds, a life-sized fisherman's kitchen, and a tapestry commemorating a disaster in 1881 when 189 fishermen were drowned in a sudden storm. And so to the border town of Berwick-upon-Tweed.

Berwick has had a chequered history and been razed or ravaged on many occasions. It is encircled by walls built by Elizabeth I, who directed her commander to 'keep this town and my kingdom safe against the Scots', only to be succeeded by Scotland's King James whose accession to the English throne made these expensive defenses unneccesary. Berwick remains a very splendid town, well worth exploring before setting off west and north across the heart of Berwickshire and Lammermuir.

From Berwick take the A6105 past the 1333 battlefield of Halidon Hill, where Edward III first tried out his archers against the Scots. This road leads beside Whiteadder Water - there is another called Blackadder further west - and so to the town of Duns. Before that though is Paxton House, off the B6461.

Paxton House stands in a 70-acre park beside the river Tweed and dates back to 1758. It was built by Patrick Home, the local laird, in anticipation of his marriage to a daughter of the King of Prussia, but the lady changed her mind and only a pair of gloves, given to Patrick as a love token, serve as a reminder of his hopes.

The house is very elegant, a creation of the Adam brothers, with plasterwork designed by Robert Adam, and much of the furniture by Thomas Chippendale. The picture gallery dates from 1811, and has recently been restored for use as a provincial display centre by the National Gallery of Scotland.

Duns is a pretty market town and in medieval times was the home of the monk John Duns Scotus, who was born there in 1266. Duns Scotus came up with a number of ideas considered so bizarre at the time that anyone who listened to them was called a 'Duns'- or dunce.

The second famous son is of a more recent date. Duns was the home of motor-racing driver Jim Clark, one of the post-war racing scene's most popular champions. Jim was killed on the track in 1968 and is commemorated in Duns by the Jim Clark Room in Newton Street, where many of his trophies and other memorabilia are on display. Jim Clark won the World Championship twice, but crashed fatally on the Hockenheim circuit on 7 April 1968. He is buried in the churchyard at Chirnside, east of Duns on the A6105.

Do not miss the castle at Hume nearby, partly because it is a good one but mainly because the countryside round about is beautiful, a patchwork of fields and woods set about with hills and empty of people. From Hume Castle turn north and follow minor roads to the town of Lauder, a first-class touring centre with walks and pony rides and cycle trips on offer into the surrounding countryside.

One of the glories of Lauder is Thirlestane Castle, built as a fort in the 13th century and developed over the centuries since. It is the home of the Maitland family who have lived here since the 16th century, and since the Maitlands are also the Earls and later Dukes of Lauderdale, their home is naturally quite splendid, though haunted by the ghost of one of the Dukes who died during the reign of Charles II.

After visiting Lauder head back down the A697 and then take the B6456 for Duns, turning left just outside the town onto the minor road across the Lammermuir Hills to Gifford and Haddington, and eventually back to Gullane. This tour covers the best parts of the coast and countryside of North Berwickshire, but don't rush it. Places like this should be savoured over a full weekend.

INFORMATION:

GULLANE LIES ON THE A198, EAST FROM EDINBURGH VIA LONGNIDDRY TOWARDS NORTH BERWICK.

GREYWALLS, MUIRFIELD, GULLANE, TEL. 0620 842144; BROWN'S HOTEL, HADDINGTON, TEL. 0620 822254. TIC (NORTH BERWICK), TEL. 0620 2197; TIC (BERWICK-UPON-TWEED), TEL. 0289 330733.

28

North Norfolk Coast

—

Up here on the breezy Norfolk coast lie fine towns like King's Lynn and Cromer, fortresses like Castle Rising, Royal homes like Sandringham and places of pilgrimage like Walsingham. To these can be added a clutch of attractive villages, good walks and ample opportunities for outdoor activities such as birdwatching and golf. My choice for a base lies between the little port of Cley-next-the-Sea, and the village of Grimston, near King's Lynn. This region can be bleak in winter, but is just about perfect in the other seasons of the year.

King's Lynn is 110 miles from London, 120 miles from Birmingham, and 130 miles from Leeds.

Norfolk has never quite recovered from Noel Coward's dismissive remark, 'Very flat, Norfolk', during the balcony scene in *Private Lives*. In fact Norfolk is not very flat and this northern part, east of King's Lynn, rolls a great deal, a pleasing mixture of low hills, small fields, woods and copses. North Norfolk, in short, is an attractive part of England and enjoys a fair amount of decent weather, though it can be bitter on the coast when the wind is cutting in across the North Sea.

As the first base for a weekend on the North Norfolk coast there is the Congham Hall Country House Hotel and Restaurant at Grimston, four miles east of King's Lynn. Congham Hall is a long, low, Georgian manor house set in 40 acres of park and garden, and converted into a hotel in 1982.

Congham Hall has a first-class restaurant with a good wine list. Other inducements are tours of the herb garden, a swimming pool, tennis courts, and the chance to watch cricket on the hotel's private pitch, home of the village team. If it rains there are weekend cookery courses or an impromptu day in the kitchen learning the secrets of the chef. For those who insist on going out whatever the weather, the hotel lends guests umbrellas, wellies and waterproofs.

Nearby King's Lynn is a beautiful port and a most historic town, with a lot of fine buildings around two squares known as the Saturday Market and the Tuesday Market. Half a day on foot here is barely enough time to explore the town and see the 15th-century Guildhall, the 13th-century church of St Margaret and the Bank House in Staithe Square.

After that it is time to tour, but first a word of advice: note the village signs. Many of these are real works of art, each carved and painted in a distinctive fashion. Most are puns on the village name or display the occupations of the inhabitants and are great fun to spot as you travel around.

A good tour along 40 miles of the North Norfolk coast might begin at Sandringham House, eight miles north-east of King's Lynn. Sandringham has been one of the Royal Family's favourite homes since the end of the last century. Parts of the house are open when the family is not in residence, and the gardens are open all year.

A little to the north of King's Lynn lies Castle Rising, a forbidding medieval pile where Queen Isabella, the 'She Wolf of France', was imprisoned for years by her son, Edward III. Rising is a very fine castle and well worth a visit. So too is Houghton Hall near King's Lynn, now the seat of the Marquess of Cholmondeley, an 18th-century Palladian-style mansion built by Sir Robert Walpole, with elegant rooms and a superb collection of over 20,000 model soldiers.

The sea has drawn back a little from the coast and most of the places 'next-the-sea', like Wells-next-the-Sea and Cley-next-the-Sea, are now a mile or two inland. Those who want to visit one of the small harbours should look for the word 'staithe', Old English for port or harbour, as in Burnham Overy Staithe.

There are a score of pretty places to see along this coast but do not miss Burnham Thorpe, the birthplace of Admiral Horatio Nelson, who was born here on 29 September 1758. Nelson's father was the rector

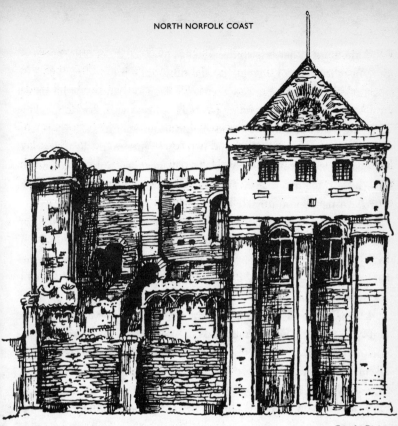

Castle Rising

of Burnham Thorpe and the church is now a naval shrine, full of Lord Nelson memorabilia.

After Burnham Thorpe comes the little town of Wells-next-the-Sea, the end of the Wells and Walsingham Light Railway - the longest narrow gauge steam railway in the world. If the trains are running, you can catch one down to Walsingham for a visit to the shrine.

The journey takes about 45 minutes and there is plenty of time to walk about Walsingham before taking another train north again. Walsingham was one of the great pilgrim centres of medieval England, a place that ranked with Canterbury before the Reformation, and it is now enjoying something of a revival. There are cafés and shops and several good pubs, but the real attraction of Walsingham is its air of spirituality.

Something rather less spiritual hangs over the quiet little village of Stiffkey, the scene of a great scandal during the inter-war years. The Vicar of Stiffkey - pronounced 'Stewkey' - took to abandoning his parish on Sunday nights and spending the bulk of his time in London, talking to young ladies of dubious virtue. After various attempts to restore him to a sense of duty had failed, the reverend gentleman was unfrocked and took to lay-preaching with a circus. All went well until he decided to preach from the lion's cage. The lion, who knew what lions have to do with Christians, promptly ate him.

Our route lies east, towards Blakeney. This is one of Norfolk's top birdwatching areas, but visitors might also enjoy the boat trip from Wells to Blakeney Point to see the seals. Otherwise press on to Cley-next-the-Sea, and to the George and Dragon Hotel which is a birdwatchers' pub and full of delights.

Like most of the pubs and restaurants along this coast, the George and Dragon specialises in crabs and other forms of seafood, which come cooked to perfection either as a bar snack or as a full meal in the restaurant. The walls are covered with photographs and notices telling of life locally, including one seeking the arrest of a highwayman known to hang out in the George and Dragon between forays up the road.

The big attraction, however, is the family Bible-sized Bird Book in the Lectern Bar. This is used by local and visiting birdwatchers to record their sightings, many of them adding pen and ink sketches of the bird in question.

Cley is a pretty little town with a lot of small shops, a windmill and houses built of stones and pebbles, set along narrow streets. It is a real fishermen's village and though popular with visitors manages to avoid being twee.

To see some of the bird life around Cley requires the local rig-of-the-day, a Barbour jacket, boots, a field guide and binoculars. Thus equipped, there are walks along the coast following two overlapping long-distance footpaths, the Peddars Way, which runs across Norfolk and along the coast, and the Norfolk Coast Path. Both provide the chance to see plenty of birds.

The Norfolk Coast Path begins at Hunstanton, the popular seaside resort north of King's Lynn, and runs east to Cromer, a distance of around 40 miles, but it can be joined at a number of places en route and is never far from the road or a village. Norfolk is, in fact, well supplied with walks and apart from these two there is the Angles Way, the Weavers Way and the Around Norfolk Walk, as well as a great variety of local footpaths.

From Cley the road runs to Sheringham, a rather up-market resort with a fine golf course, and into the town of Cromer, famous for seafood and a splendid church. In fact most of the churches of Norfolk and Suffolk are rather splendid, far too large for any current congregation and too numerous for even a percentage to be included here. A peek into one or two will certainly add pleasure to a weekend in this glorious part of England.

INFORMATION:

KING'S LYNN LIES AT THE JUNCTION OF SEVERAL MAIN ROADS: THE A10 NORTH FROM ELY, THE A148 WEST FROM FAKENHAM, THE A149 SOUTH FROM HUNSTANTON, THE A17 EAST FROM SPALDING AND HOLBEACH. WELLS-NEXT-THE-SEA IS ON THE A149 BETWEEN HUNSTANTON AND CROMER.

CONGHAM HALL COUNTRY HOUSE HOTEL, GRIMSTON, TEL. 0485 600250; THE DUKE'S HEAD HOTEL, KING'S LYNN, TEL. 0553 774996; THE GEORGE AND DRAGON HOTEL, CLEY-NEXT-THE-SEA, TEL. 0263 740652. TIC (KING'S LYNN), TEL. 0553 763044; TIC (HUNSTANTON), TEL. 0485 532610; TIC (WELLS-NEXT-THE-SEA), TEL. 0328 710885.

Otmoor

*England is full of quiet, out of the way places, if you only know where to look.
One of the quietest lies just north-west of the city of Oxford, where half a
dozen pretty villages surround the green and level basin of Otmoor. Otmoor
is a little dream, blessed with two good hotels and well supplied with country pubs, a place of fields and flowers, seamed with peaceful lanes and
footpaths. The moor is delightful at any time but is particularly lovely in the
spring, or in the autumn when the hedgerows are full of blackberries, hips
and haws.*

*Otmoor is 60 miles from London, 65 miles from Birmingham, and 75
miles from Bristol.*

At the end of the last century, the
ditches and fields of Otmoor gave the writer Lewis Carroll the idea for the
chessboard in *Alice Through the Looking Glass*, written in the village of
Beckley, which overlooks Otmoor from the south.

Otmoor is a peaceful place, ideal for a writer, a honeymoon couple
or people on a weekend break. The bustle of 'Town and Gown' in
Oxford seems a million miles away and the sound of traffic pouring
down the M40 to the east cannot be heard on the moor. There are no
roads running directly across the moor today, though according to the OS
map, a road ran right across it from Oxford, up through the village of
Murcott to Bicester and beyond, in Roman times.

Today only quiet country lanes circle the moor and those who wish to
get across it must go on foot along the many paths that join the little villages
round the rim. Many of the country lanes are linked into the Oxfordshire
Cycleway, so those who have bikes might like to put them in the back of the
car for half a day's cycling around this tranquil - and flat - countryside.

Apart from lavish amounts of peace and quiet, the great attraction of Otmoor is the small villages around the edge, each with a pleasant pub - like the thatched George at Stanton St John, a stone-built village where the houses are draped in honeysuckle. From Stanton St John there is a good half-hour footpath walk to the White Hart at Forest Hill, another flower-decorated hamlet. Even more heavily festooned with flowers is The Plough at Noke, a tiny village on the moor south of Islip, right at the end of a lane.

The Plough is small and full of locals but press on for another hundred yards to the tiny church of St Giles, which is Early English, dating from 1086, topped by an open belfry and containing a font presented to the church by the Lady Gundreda, William the Conqueror's daughter. There is also the tomb of Benedict Winchcombe, who died in 1623 but still haunts the village on winter nights, accompanied by a pack of hounds.

Noke has retained its old village schoolhouse, complete with bell to summon the children to class, and this is a good place to start a walk across the moor on the Oxfordshire Way, a long-distance footpath which appears all over Otmoor. The path is easy to follow; but from any of the villages an hour's tramp in any direction will take the walker to one of the other villages, or as they are known locally, the 'Seven Towns of Otmoor'. They all have something to offer.

Islip, which lies on a low hill above the River Ray, a tributary of the Cherwell, once belonged to the Bishop of Oxford and is another place with a fine church and lots of narrow streets and lanes lined with attractive cottages and gardens; just the place for a quiet evening stroll before a drink at The Swan by the bridge, or the Red Lion in the centre.

Charlton-on-Otmoor has the Crown Inn and a remarkably fine church, where by long tradition the box-wood cross over the rood screen is renewed twice a year, on 1 May and 19 September. There is also some handsome blazonry in the chancel windows displaying the arms of Richard II, Edward III and Joanna of Navarre, wife of Henry IV. The latter is curious because Queen Joanna was generally believed to be a witch.

Beckley, where Carroll wrote about Alice, has a wonderful church, a good inn for lunch, and is said to be one of the prettiest villages in Oxfordshire. Built in that attractive silver stone so common hereabouts, it also has splendid views over the moor. The church, built from about 1150, is endowed with a 'squint', a large peephole through the wall of the chancel through which the common folk in the nave could watch the priest at the altar.

As a base for all this there is a choice of historic hotels. The Studley Priory Hotel is situated in a former Benedictine nunnery dating back to the time of Richard Coeur-de-Lion and set in 13 acres of wooded garden, with remarkable views over the moor and the Oxfordshire plain. From the Dissolution of the Monasteries in 1539 until 1877, Studley belonged to the Croke family. Charles I stayed there during the Civil War and the priory has been a hotel since the 1960s.

There is a great deal of Victorian wood panelling in the bar, several Tudor bedrooms complete with four-posters, comfortable public rooms and good food. The hotel also offers activity weekends: clay pigeon shooting on the lawn, horse-riding from nearby stables, or golf lessons at the Southfield Golf Club.

The Weston Manor Hotel is at Weston-on-the-Green, a mile north of the moor, just off the M40 at Exit 9. Weston-on-the-Green is a lovely village going back to Saxon times, though the present manor dates from the 16th century when it belonged to Henry VIII and then to the Norreys and Bertie families, who became Earls of Berkshire and of Abingdon respectively. The Manor has been a hotel since 1983.

The house is a fine Tudor mansion, standing in broad acres, with all the comforts of a modern hotel. These include a heated swimming pool, croquet on the lawn and a squash court. The hotel is handsomely furnished and the fittings include an 'Act of Parliament' clock, one of the clocks introduced to taverns and public buildings after William Pitt imposed a tax on private time-pieces in 1797 to help finance the war against Napoleon. Everyone promptly got rid of their own clocks and watches, so pubs installed these 'Act of Parliament' clocks to help their customers tell the time.

'Act of Parliament' clock

As a final inducement to visit the Manor there is also a resident ghost. This is in the shape of 'Mad Maude', a young nun who was burned at the stake in the manor grounds for being over friendly with some, or maybe all, of the resident monks, back in the Middle Ages.

The great appeal of Otmoor is its tranquillity, the charming villages, the friendly pubs, beautiful countryside and fine walks; but if this is still not enough, there are plenty of good excursions to sights round about.

The city of Oxford lies just seven miles from the moor and offers more history, tours of the colleges - including the grounds and deer park of Magdalen College - as well as excellent shopping, cinemas and theatres. Nine miles to the north-west on the A44 lies Woodstock, another pretty and very historic town.

Woodstock was once a Royal Manor - the Black Prince was born there - but in 1704 the manor of Woodstock was given by Queen Anne to her most successful general, John Churchill, Duke of Marlborough. Churchill's great house, Blenheim Palace, is the chief attraction of Woodstock, and should not be missed on any visit to the area.

Winston Churchill was born at Blenheim (and is buried in the family plot at nearby Bladon) and an exhibition of Winston memorabilia is a feature of the palace, which is anyway magnificent, as are the park and grounds which surround it. Woodstock town centre contains the

CountyMuseum and the 13th-century Bear Hotel, another medieval hostelry which serves a good Sunday lunch.

Before that, though, you might fancy a drink on the riverside terrace of The Trout at Godstow near Wolvercote, just to the north of Oxford. That is, if you can tear yourself away from Otmoor, the perfect place for a country weekend.

INFORMATION:

OTMOOR LIES JUST NORTH AND EAST OF THE B4027, WHICH LINKS THE A40 AND A34 NORTH-EAST OF THE CITY OF OXFORD.

STUDLEY PRIORY HOTEL, HORTON-CUM-STUDLEY, TEL. 0865 351203; WESTON MANOR HOTEL, WESTON-ON-THE-GREEN, TEL. 0869 50621; THE BEAR HOTEL, WOODSTOCK, TEL. 0993 811511. TIC (WOODSTOCK); TEL. 0993 811038; TIC (OXFORD), TEL. 0865 726871.

30

Pendle Hill and the Forest of Bowland

—

Pendle is in the Ribble Valley, close to the Forest of Bowland, in the central part of Lancashire. Set around the market town of Clitheroe, it is a region of rushing rivers, wide valleys and rolling hills, largely free of tourists but well endowed with small villages and an assortment of friendly northern pubs.

Clitheroe is 40 miles from Manchester, 45 miles from Leeds, 110 miles from Newcastle, and 125 miles from Birmingham.

This part of England owes what fame it has to a writer, though like the area itself, this writer is not as well known as he should be. The Brontes, James Herriot and Beatrix Potter have all done their best for the north. But few have done it so well as Robert Neill, whose classic tale, *Mist Over Pendle*, a story of witchcraft and romance, is a splendid evocation of this beautiful and mysterious country. A copy of *Mist Over Pendle* is almost indispensable on this weekend break.

The other essential element is a good hotel. As a base for the region there is the Northcote Manor hotel at Langho, near Blackburn, which lies out in the countryside under the loom of Pendle Hill. The proprietors are keen that their visitors should get out and about to enjoy all that is on offer, so maps and guidebooks are produced on arrival.

Northcote Manor is overlooked by the great bulk of Pendle Hill, the trysting ground in the 17th century of the Pendle witches, who put a terrible fear into the local people until they were eventually hunted down by Roger Nowell, the local magistrate, tried at Lancaster in 1610 and hanged on a triangular gibbet outside the town.

Even after three and a half centuries the witches cast a spell over Pendle Hill. The local shops feature them in the story-book fashion, hook-nosed crones who rode broomsticks and went about with cats, but the actual witches were far more sinister, given to blackmail and murder.

However, before looking for witches there is the market town of Clitheroe, which has a castle, a twice-weekly market that dates back to the Middle Ages, and at least two shops of particular interest. The first of these is Brynes Wine Store in the High Street, a vast place with deep cellars stocking over 1,200 different kinds of wine, including a lot of New World wines and vintages from such unlikely countries as Wales and India.

The second attraction is Cowman's Pie Shop, across the way, a family-run concern specialising in home-prepared food from old recipes, with such rare delights as bacon and egg sausages - each a breakfast in itself - or hand-raised pies or sage and onion sausages. For a small town Clitheroe offers a great variety of good shopping and the shopkeepers, like most northern folk, are remarkably friendly to visitors.

Another place well worth visiting is the Pendle Antiques Centre at Sabden, south of Clitheroe in the Forest of Pendle. This describes itself as 'Probably the most interesting place to visit in the area', and for lovers of antiques it lives up to that claim. The Centre covers three floors and contains everything from books and sideboards to rugs and jewellery.

Good maps and guides to the area can be found in the Kaydee Bookshop in Moor Lane, Clitheroe, which has been voted the Best Independent Bookshop in Britain and, equipped with a local map and guide, it is time to go walking, or touring by car or bicycle.

One of the main excursions on foot has to be the ascent of Pendle Hill, which lies due east of Clitheroe and at 1,827ft (557m) is not quite high enough to be a mountain.

The best place to start an ascent, for which a fit walker should allow two to three hours, is the pretty village of Newchurch in Pendle, just south of the hill, a place which features often in *Mist Over Pendle*. The witches came here to desecrate the graves and the leader of the coven, Alice Nutter, who was one of those hanged at Lancaster, lived at Roughlee nearby.

Mist Over Pendle, first published in 1951, is still in print (Arrow Books) but not all that easy to come by outside Pendle, where most of the shops hold a few copies. Pendle Hill does offer other attractions apart from creepy tales, like hang-gliding and dry-skiing, but the walking is superb and the views from the top quite exceptional.

Other places within easy reach include the Yorkshire Dales National Park; Stonyhurst, a public school set in magnificent grounds; the Martin Mere Wildfowl Trust; a number of stately homes like Gawthorpe Hall; and ruined abbeys like the one at Sawley, just to the north of Clitheroe.

Another attraction is the Museum of Childhood at Ribchester which contains a comprehensive collection of teddy bears, a flea circus, a carousel, toy soldiers and all manner of other exhibits; a real treat for kids of all ages. Full details on all these places can be obtained from the TIC in Clitheroe.

The main footpath hereabouts is the Ribble Way, but one of the easiest and most enjoyable local walks is from village to village along the Ribble Valley through some of the places mentioned in *Mist Over Pendle*. Given a 1:50.000 scale OS map it is easy to walk up the valley from Newchurch in Pendle to Barley, Roughlee and Blacko, and so up Weets Hill.

Those who enjoy pleasant villages can mark some of the following on a map and use them as points of interest on a car tour. White-well, north-west of Clitheroe, is set in such tumbled country that they call it 'Little

Fairy Bridge, Ribble Valley

Switzerland', and the Inn at Whitewell is good for a stop. Slaidburn on

the B6478 is a fine village with an equally fine and popular inn, the Hark to Bounty - named after a favourite hound of a 19th-century hunting squire, Parson Wigglesworth.

The inn was once the medieval courtroom for the district and those found guilty of dreadful crimes like stealing the King's Deer were promptly strung up from the rafters; the grooves made by the ropes can still be seen on the beams. The Sun Inn at Chipping, near Longridge Fell, is said to be haunted.

Waddington is by repute the prettiest village in the district, though my vote goes to Whalley, south of Clitheroe, not least for the ruins of the 13th-century Cistercian abbey, destroyed at the Reformation. Here too is Foxfields Hotel, with a nine-hole golf course.

One could spend an entire and rewarding weekend in the Ribble Valley, with Pendle Hill to provide a backdrop. But it would be a shame to visit Pendle without taking a drive through the pass of the Trough of Bowland, and over the fells to the historic city of Lancaster.

The Forest of Bowland is a region of mixed forest, moors and fells, marvellously wild and quite deserted except for the sheep that seem to thrive in this bleak environment. There are very few roads across it and the main one is simply a moorland track, somewhat narrow but quite passable, from Newton on the B6478 north of Clitheroe, all the way to Lancaster, past Whins Brow and Sykes Fell, rising up to some 1,500ft (457m) at the crest before falling off into the western valley.

Lancaster, on the River Lune, has a medieval castle that doubled as a prison and court house, an 18th-century Customs House, a lot of Georgian buildings and more than a few good pubs. After a look at all that there is the drive back over the moors to Langho, and if the moon is up, Pendle Hill will be standing out against the night sky, a reminder of witches and wild times long ago.

INFORMATION:

CLITHEROE LIES ON THE A59 BETWEEN JUNCTION 31 ON THE M6 (PRESTON) AND SKIPTON.

NORTHCOTE MANOR, LANGHO, TEL. 0254 240555; FOXFIELDS HOTEL, WHALLEY,

TEL. 0254 822556. TIC (CLITHEROE), TEL. 0200 25566.

31

Petworth

The old market town of Petworth in the heart of Sussex is an ideal centre for a weekend break, with a wealth of antique shops, some good hotels and restaurants, and plenty to see in the countryside round about. The sea is no great distance away and as a central attraction there is Petworth House, one of the great country houses of England. This is a year-round destination, with something to see and do in every season.

Petworth is 50 miles from London, 120 miles from Bristol, and 150 miles from Birmingham.

Petworth is an old town and it shows. The centre is small, a maze of little streets and squares, lined with small, cosy, red-brick houses, some Tudor but most from the 18th century, huddled together below the walls of Petworth House. William Cobbett described Petworth as 'a nice market town, but solid and clean...everything of the building kind has an air of great strength and produces the agreeable idea of durability'.

Petworth has certainly endured. The town was listed in the Domesday Book and the centre is still unspoiled by modern developments. The parish church of St Mary the Virgin was built in the 14th century, and although rebuilt in the early 19th century, it has an ancient air and is full of memorials.

Most visitors to Petworth concentrate on Petworth House but the town itself is well worth exploring. Parking is difficult, so the best way to get around the town is on foot. There is a free car park right by the Tourist Information Centre, and if the TIC is shut, there is a useful information post, plastered with maps and good advice, at the top of the car park.

From there a covered shopping mall leads out to Golden Square, past Blackbirds Bookshop, another place full of helpful information, books and local maps. Tucked into a corner of the square is the New Star pub, which does good lunches, but the big attraction of a stroll round Petworth is the antique shops.

The current promoters of Petworth refer to the town as 'The Antique Centre of the South'. Every other shop seems to sell antiques, while the Petworth Antique Market in East Street contains no less than 35 separate dealers, all anxious to sell their wares. The non-antique shops are of the market-town variety, a couple of good wine merchants, a boutique or two, a delicatessen, and several good teashops.

My special place in Petworth is Lombard Steet, an ancient, narrow, cobbled street running from the market square to St Mary's church; it provides the perfect photo-opportunity at the top, where St Mary's is framed by the old buildings at the end of the street. Lombard Street is at least 300 years old and was once the main thoroughfare leading to Petworth House.

Petworth House made Petworth famous, for the house and the deer park which surrounds it are both remarkable. The park dates from 1752 and is a creation of Lancelot 'Capability' Brown, who was then at the height of his powers. The park now contains a herd of 400 fallow deer, covers an area of 2,000 acres (750 of which belong to the National Trust) and is enclosed by a wall 13 miles long.

All the great architects of the English country house came to work at Petworth. *Michelin* describes it as 'The nearest thing to a Louis XIV château in England', and though it can hardly outrank Vaux in the Ile de France, it is certainly very splendid, especially seen from across the lake.

Petworth House was built at the end of the 17th century by Charles Seymour, 6th Duke of Somerset. The south front looks towards the South Downs and the rooms contain carvings by Grinling Gibbons and the largest collection of paintings by Turner, who often visited the great house to paint, outside the Tate Gallery. There is also the magnificent Grand Staircase and, among the art collection, works by Van Dyck, Reynolds, Kneller, Bosch and Lely. A tour of Petworth House, followed by a walk in the deer park, is part of any visit to the area.

A wander round Petworth Park will take a couple of hours, but those who fancy more of a challenge can try a stretch of the South Downs Way along the top of the Downs, or ramble along the Downs Link Walk, the long-distance footpath which links the South Downs Way with the North Downs Way.

Those who stay at the Little Thakeham Hotel at Storrington during their visit to the Petworth area have an advantage, for the owners will drive dedicated walkers up to the South Downs Way and pick them up at some pre-arranged point. For something rather less energetic, I recommend finding a short walk on the local OS map with a pub at the end of it.

Petworth House

Petworth has one good small hotel, the historic Angel, on the road out to Fittleworth, within walking distance of the town centre. The pub is medieval but the name goes back to the Pilgrim Fathers who, when forced to leave England to seek religious freedom, made their way across country to Southampton. Not every hostelry welcomed them, but to those which did they gave the name 'Angel', and in Petworth the name endures. Another pub recommended by Petworth people is the Horseguards Inn at Tillington, a mile or so from the town.

Petworth is surrounded by good hotels. Among these is another Angel Hotel, seven miles away at Midhurst, a 16th-century coaching inn, noted for comfortable rooms and very good food. Indeed, the great attraction of this Angel is the food. The hotel has won the Country Restaurant of the Year award and has many other commendations, not least an enthusiastic local clientele.

The Little Thakeham Hotel at Storrington, about seven miles southeast of Petworth, beyond Pulborough, has just nine rooms, but the food is good, with seafood from Selsey and South Downs lamb as two particular specialities.

The other feature of Little Thakeham is the garden, which has been restored in the style of Gertrude Jekyll. The owners have spent a small fortune doing it, and those people who don't stay at the hotel should drop in perhaps for a meal and take a look at the garden.

With the town and environs of Petworth fully explored, the time has come for a look at some of the attractions further afield. The winery at Lurgashall, six miles north of the town, is worth inspection; Midhurst has polo at Cowdray Park and a fine golf course; and there is park-and-play golf available at Osiers Farm Golf Course, two miles north of Petworth.

Arundel, 11 miles south of Petworth, is a historic town, full of attractions. Most obvious of these is Arundel Castle, home of the Duke of Norfolk, the premier Catholic layman in England. Arundel is one of the finest and best-preserved medieval castles in the country.

The gatehouse dates from the 12th century and the public rooms contain works by Kneller and Van Dyck, Gainsborough and Reynolds.

Arundel Cathedral looks very splendid, but the Fitzalan Chapel at the east end of the parish church is the place to see, filled as it is with the tombs of the Howards. This is a very unusual church because the nave belongs to the town and is therefore Protestant-Anglican, while the Fitzalan Chapel belongs to the Dukes of Norfolk and thus is Catholic.

A mile north of Arundel is the Wildfowl and Wetlands Trust, one of the finest bird reserves in the south of England, with a Visitors' Centre, a licensed restaurant and a host of ducks, geese and swans. To the north-west of there, on the A286, is the Weald and Downland Open Air Museum at Singleton, where more than 30 historic rural buildings have been re-erected to form a display of vernacular architecture, including a mill and a village school.

Petworth, Arundel and Chichester, all hold summer festivals between July and September. For evening entertainment there is the Chichester Festival Theatre, one of the finest regional theatres in the country, with productions to match. Then there is Goodwood House, and the racecourse, Glyndbourne and the Sussex coast, all in easy reach. One weekend in Petworth will not be enough to see it all.

INFORMATION:

PETWORTH LIES ON THE A272 BETWEEN MIDHURST AND BILLINGSHURST, AT THE JUNCTION WITH THE A283 FROM MILFORD TO PULBOROUGH.

ANGEL HOTEL, PETWORTH, TEL. 0798 42153; ANGEL HOTEL, MIDHURST, TEL. 0730 812421; LITTLE THAKEHAM HOTEL, STORRINGTON, TEL. 0903 744416. TIC (ARUNDEL), TEL. 0903 882268; TIC (CHICHESTER), TEL. 0243 775888.

32

Richmond and the Yorkshire Dales

—

The fortress town of Richmond has been overshadowed by the charms and attractions of York, that mecca for anyone visiting what we are now urged to call the 'White Rose County'.

This is a pity, for Richmond, set on a bluff above the River Swale, is a rather splendid town with a fine castle. There are lots of attractions within the town itself, and Richmond is an excellent touring base for the Yorkshire Dales and the Herriot Country which lie just to the east.

Richmond is 45 miles from Newcastle, 50 miles from Leeds, and 105 miles from Manchester.

Richmond town and castle should be considered together since they were built as one around 1071, soon after the Norman Conquest, as part of William the Conqueror's attempts to quell rebellions in the north.

The present castle, an imposing structure with a 100ft-high (30m) keep, was built in the 12th century and remained a bastion of the north throughout the Middle Ages. In fact the castle had a somewhat tranquil existence; no great battles or sieges took place here and most of the interior and curtain walls are still as they were at the end of the 16th century, with only natural decay and the effects of time contributing to any deterioration. The castle is now in the hands of English Heritage, who have roofed and restored the Great Hall to give a fair idea of what life must have been like in a medieval castle; cold, damp and draughty.

For a touch of comfort there is the King's Head Hotel, a fine example of an 18th-century coaching inn, looking out on the market place with views towards the castle and the tall eroded obelisk, erected in 1771 to replace the original Market Cross. The town was granted a charter for a market in the 12th century and there is still a market on Saturday mornings.

Holy Trinity church in the centre of the market place was founded by the Normans but has experienced a number of role changes down the centuries, as a school, prison and warehouse. Part of it was a shop when it ceased to be a church in 1971.

It now contains the Regimental Museum of the Green Howards, one of the distinguished Yorkshire regiments. This regiment was formed in 1688 and has recruited in Richmond and the country round about for the last 300 years. The museum contains a fascinating collection of weapons and uniforms, records the regiment's 18 VCs and details its

Richmond Castle

exploits in the Crimea and all the many wars since. The museum also contains the regimental archives and the town collection of civic silver. Although military museums are not to everyone's taste, this one is worth a visit.

From the large market place a maze of streets and alleyways, or wynds, meander through the town. Friars Wynd leads to the parish church of St Mary, which contains the Memorial Chapel of the Green Howards. This church dates from the 12th century, but was restored in the last century by Sir Gilbert Scott. The wynd takes its name from the Franciscan friars who lived in 'Greyfriars' in what is now Queen's Road, though of their former friary only a tower remains.

Richmond is a 'strolling' town and places to see include the Georgian Theatre Royal, which was built in 1788 and served as wine vaults, an auction room and a corn chandler's before being restored to its original purpose and splendour in the 1960s. Great players like Edmund Kean and Sarah Siddons have performed at the Theatre Royal in Richmond, and the theatre still operates today with a full programme of plays, shows and recitals. There is also a museum devoted to theatrical life.

Although the castle, the Green Howards museum and the Theatre Royal are the principal attractions of Richmond, these are complemented by plenty of other curious or interesting places dotted about the streets of the town, each identified by a plaque and traceable via a leaflet from the Tourist Information Centre.

Through Frenchgate Bar on the north side of the market place the trail leads into a street called the Great Channel, where Charles Dodgson, better known as Lewis Carroll, once went to school. Frenchgate has some fine Georgian houses, and the trail then leads on to the Richmondshire Museum off Ryders Wynd. Richmondshire is an addition to the English counties and the museum is full of local history, with displays of crafts, toys, farming implements, photographs and - a new one this - some of the sets from the television series *All Creatures Great and Small*, the stories of James Herriot, a local vet.

There are some good walks along the River Swale including one to the ruins of Easby Abbey, a 12th-century Cistercian foundation a mile or so outside the town. Otherwise, with Richmond explored, it is time to get into the car and drive west for a tour of the Dales and Herriot Country.

One of the terrors of the literary life must be when fiction becomes confused with reality and one's work becomes the basis of a tourist trail. In the case of James Herriot this growing practice has advantages, for the stories are set in the glorious countryside of Swaledale, Wensleydale and Arkengarthdale, and finding the places referred to adds an extra dimension to a journey around the region.

The A6108/B6270 route from Richmond to Reeth has been described as 'the most beautiful road in England', which may well be true. Stop at the hill near the youth hostel at Grinton, which offers marvellous views over Swaledale and Arkengarthdale and see for yourself.

The Swaledale Folk Museum in Reeth is worth inspection, and if the bridge over Arkle Beck looks familiar that is because it was used for the opening shots in the Herriot TV series. Reeth has a number of attractive Georgian houses, a good pub at the King's Arms and a wonderful view down the valley towards Grinton and Fremington Edge. This is the heart of Swaledale, a place of small fields set about with greystone walls, rolling hills and open sky; quite delightful.

From here the road out of Swaledale and into Wensleydale leads through Muker over the Buttertubs Pass. At Keld, just north of Muker, a minor road climbs to the Tan Hill Inn on Arkengarthdale Moor, one of the highest situated inns in England, with more of those spectacular views.

If lunchtime is approaching, the road south from Muker leads through Simonstone and Hardraw into Hawes. The church at Hardraw features on television as the church of 'Darrowby', while 'Darrowby Cattle Market' is composed of various parts of the market town of Hawes. The Green Dragon pub in Hawes does a good bar lunch, as does the Simonstone Hall Country House Hotel.

Follow the road to Bainbridge from Hawes through Wensleydale into the village of Askrigg, which plays the part of 'Darrowby' in the series. Sights to see here are the fine parish church and the King's Arms

Hotel, also known as the Darrowby 'Drovers Arms'. All these villages have pleasant small hotels and inns where the landlords will serve coffee, tea or meals, as well as hard liquor.

Castle Bolton, further on down the road back to Richmond, has a history which predates the television age; Mary, Queen of Scots was imprisoned in Bolton Castle, and you can see her bedchamber there. Then comes the village of Wensley from which Wensleydale takes its name, and so back onto the A6108 to return to Richmond.

This route through Herriot Country is not very long, less than 50 miles, but with stops and diversions it would be as well to allow half a day. Nor is there any need to get overly involved in the doings of those fictional vets. The Herriot tales are a peg to hang the trip on, nothing more. But this short drive covers some of the grandest scenery in Yorkshire, and is worth taking on that account alone.

INFORMATION:

RICHMOND LIES JUST WEST OF THE A1 ON THE A6136 NORTH FROM CATTERICK, FOUR MILES SOUTH-WEST OF SCOTCH CORNER.

THE KING'S HEAD HOTEL, RICHMOND, TEL. 0748 850220; SIMONSTONE HALL HOTEL, HAWES, TEL. 0969 667255. TIC (RICHMOND), TEL. 0748 850252/825994.

33

Ruthin and Snowdonia

—

Those Britons who want to visit another country without actually going abroad need look no further than North Wales and Snowdonia. Here the Welsh tongue is still in everyday use and the people who speak it slip easily in and out of English, just to help the foreigner from across the frontier feel a little more at home. North Wales has some exciting scenery and a variety of attractions and activities, many of them close to the ancient market town of Ruthin.

Ruthin is 60 miles from Manchester, 90 miles from Birmingham, and 155 miles from Cardiff.

For natural attractions North Wales can offer the coast of the Irish Sea and the hill-country of Snowdonia, the two linked by a series of river valleys running inland from the sea. Dotted about among the hills are a number of attractive places and lots of splendid castles, most of them relics of the many attempts made by Edward I to subdue the Welsh and extend his dominion to the Irish Sea.

Conwy, Harlech, Caernarfon, Beaumaris on the Isle of Anglesey, Denbigh, Criccieth and Ruthin all have castles built to the orders of Edward I. They are well worth a visit, and will provide the historically-minded visitor with a theme for the trip.

Ruthin, the base for this weekend, is a pretty market town on a hilltop, a place of small squares and small pubs, with a lot of good small shops and a substantial craft centre which also contains the TIC. The Welsh language is much in evidence hereabouts and visitors will soon get used to it and enjoy its pleasant lilting tones.

As a place to stay there is Ruthin Castle, a fine hotel in what was the 13th-century castle that once dominated the town. The hotel has

30 acres of garden to wander in, and 12 miles of private fishing on the nearby River Clwyd. There is also a good restaurant and for those who want a little historic fun, the merriment of a medieval Welsh banquet. Those who fancy something quieter can visit the Myddleton Arms pub in the square, just opposite the old Manor Courthouse which was built in 1401 and now contains a bank.

Another place worth visiting before setting off on tour is the Ruthin Craft Centre in Park Road. Here picture-framing, folk art, pewter-smithing, sculpting, glass-blowing and printmaking are all practised by local artists who will demonstrate their skills - and let you buy the finished products.

Ruthin lies to the east of the Snowdonia massif and the easiest way to get to the area is to skirt south on the A494 and A5 to Betws-y-Coed; but to sample a cross section of this countryside my advice is to head north up the Clwyd valley to Rhyl. Rhyl is a seaside resort overcrowded with trippers, but the way there is beautiful, with the Clwydian range to the east offering good local walks from a score of villages and the cathedral 'city' of St Asaph (pop: 3,000) as a central gem in the valley floor. The small cathedral, remodelled by Gilbert Scott in the Victorian era, is well worth a look before pressing on past Rhuddlan, which has another castle, and so up to the coast.

This north coast of Wales is lined with resorts, each a lung for the industrial cities of the north-west. Rhyl has a Suncentre and an Ocean Beach Amusement Park and miles of beach, but you may prefer the resort of Llandudno which lies further to the west between the gaunt headlands of Great Ormes Head and Little Ormes Head. These protect the beach and the pier and set off the great line of hotels, with names like the Imperial and the Hydro. Llandudno has entertainment and walks along the Prom and a cable-car ride up to Great Ormes Head, a breezy sheer-sided promontory which, apart from views over the Irish Sea, has a dry ski slope and some splendid walks.

Llandudno is full of hotels and restaurants and is a good place for lunch before crossing the river to the town of Conwy, a place guarded by one of Edward's castles. This is a mighty stronghold with eight drum towers and imposing battlements. Conwy town is also walled, but among the great sights here are the tubular railway bridge built by Robert Stephenson in 1848 and the suspension bridge constructed over the river in 1826 by Thomas Telford, in a style which chimes in with the crenellations of the nearby castle.

The Conwy valley runs inland from here for 15 miles to Betws-y-Coed, and the peaks of Snowdonia are now in sight to the west. Those who want to explore this part of North Wales could stay at the elegant Bodysgallen Hall, a country house hotel just south of Llandudno, which has extensive grounds, a croquet lawn, an obelisk on the hill, very comfortable accommodation and a good restaurant.

The Vale of Conwy is a beautiful spot, with waterfalls running down the western hillsides from the moors below the Carnedd peaks. This is good walking country with plenty of waymarked footpaths; but this is also North Wales and any walker venturing out of the valley needs boots, a map and compass, and some sensible raingear for those sudden showers.

On the way south a place which every garden lover should visit is Bodnant Garden, a National Trust property at Tal-y-Cafn, just south of Conwy. This is best visited at the end of spring when the rhododendrons and magnolias are in full bloom. There is also the famous Laburnum Arch, which is at its most glorious in late May-early June; while in autumn the fall colours on the trees are a marvel.

Betws-y-Coed is a centre for walkers and climbers who foray out from here to explore the walks and climbs available along the Llanberis Pass, or in the ranges of the Carnedds and the Glyders, which lie on either side of the road up to Bangor via Capel Curig. The less energetic

Pony-trekking in North Wales

will simply enjoy some of the finest scenery in Britain, or the wide selection of pubs and teashops that seem to abound in the towns and villages that shelter in the valleys. Pretty Llanrwst has a teashop which appears to be held together with flame-red virginia creeper, and those who fancy something rather stronger can find friendly company and good ale at the Miner's Bridge Inn in Betws-y-Coed.

Natural attractions and castles are not all that this part of North Wales has to offer. There is a vast range of outdoor activities, from fishing and pony-trekking to mountain-biking, hang-gliding and white water canoeing, a sport that is as much fun to watch as it is to do; maybe more. Caernafon, which lies to the west of Snowdon, has another castle, but also offers flights over the mountains from the local airport, and has an excellent Air Museum.

If the weather is fine and looks set to stay that way the ascent of Snowdon (3,569ft/1,087m) is one of the excursions not to be missed. Those who don't want to walk can reach the summit on the Mountain Railway from Llanberis. Otherwise there is the A5 to follow on the easy run west over the bridge and the Menai Strait onto the Isle of Anglesey, and an almost obligatory stop at the tongue-twisting village of Llanfairpwllgwyngyllgogerychwyrndrobwllllantysiliogogogoch, the longest place name in Britain. It may be wise to settle for just LlanfairPG.

Snowdonia, the North Wales coast and Ruthin have so much that one weekend will not be enough to see more than a part of it. This account has not included places like Denbigh and the wonderful car ride over the Horseshoe Pass to Valle Crucis Abbey and Llangollen, or a dozen other sights that ache to be seen. Even so, following this route and stopping off at the places mentioned here will certainly give any first-time visitor a good view of the area, and the desire to come again.

INFORMATION:

RUTHIN LIES AT THE JUNCTION OF THE A525 BETWEEN WREXHAM AND DENBIGH AND THE A494 BETWEEN BALA AND MOLD.

RUTHIN CASTLE, RUTHIN, TEL. 08242 2664; BODYSGALLEN HALL, LLANDUDNO, TEL. 0492 584466. TIC (RUTHIN), TEL. 0824 703992.

34

Sandwich and the East Coast of Kent

—

This weekend takes place in the 'Garden of England', that triangle of land between the towns of Dover, Canterbury and Sandwich, on the tip of Kent. Here there are all the requirements for a very enjoyable weekend with Sandwich, a historic town full of character and set about with golf courses, as the base.

Sandwich is 75 miles from London.

Sandwich is one of the best-preserved medieval towns in England. It is a Cinque Port, one of those places which gained special favours from the medieval monarchs in return for providing them with ships and crews.

In the Middle Ages, Sandwich thrived. In *Le Morte d'Arthur* Sir Thomas Malory names Sandwich as the premier port of the realm, and throughout history a stream of notables landed here. St Augustine passed through on his mission to the Angles. Thomas à Becket came ashore at Sandwich in 1170, a few days before his martyrdom in Canterbury Cathedral; the stairway he entered by is still known as Becket's Steps. Henry VIII came to the town to inspect his fleet anchored off the Downs, as did his daughter Elizabeth I in 1588, the year of the Armada.

Charles II returned to his kingdom via the port of Sandwich in 1660, and was welcomed by the mayor in The Bell Hotel just across from the old quay. The diarist Samuel Pepys, no stranger to the court of King Charles, was MP for Sandwich in the 1680s; and Thomas Paine, author of *The Rights of Man* and one of the architects of the American Revolution, was married in St Peter's church. Another distinguished local was John Montagu, 4th Earl of Sandwich, who by having his meal served between two slices of bread to avoid leaving the gambling table, invented the 'sandwich'.

Just wandering about the streets here can be entertaining, for it is hard not to like a place where the lanes have names like Galliard Street, Holy Ghost Alley and Moat Sole, or where one street is called The Chain, because it is exactly one pre-decimal chain long (66ft/20m).

Every ancient location in the town has a 'story board' outside. One recounts how the mayor was elected by acclaim from the citizens and forced to serve, not least because should he refuse, the citizens had the right to burn his house down.

Virtually a whole day could be spent in Sandwich wandering about the streets or around the walls and ramparts, reading the history of the town on the display boards. As a base there is The Bell Hotel on The Quay by the River Stour, a rather grand and very comfortable hotel, popular with golfers who come to play on the three championship courses outside the town. The hotel dates from the early part of the 17th century, and has a dining room overlooking the river.

Wrapped within medieval ramparts, Sandwich is a town to stroll about in, and a good way to see it all is to follow the waymarked Town Trail. There are some worthy pubs, notably the Red Cow, which has a life-sized red-painted plaster cow on the facade, the King's Arms by St Mary's church and the Admiral Owen by the toll bridge.

The town is a maze of narrow streets and alleys, lined with half-timbered houses which overhang the pavements and are themselves hung about with baskets of flowers. There is a noticeable absence of litter and graffiti, and even the newer buildings seem to blend in well with the medieval whole.

With the river silted up and used only by pleasure craft, the chief industry of the town is golf. The Royal St George's, Prince's and the Royal Cinque Ports Golf Club are championship courses which play host to events like the PGA and the British Open.

Walks available include the five-to-six-mile hike from Sandwich to Deal along the coast, which will take about three hours; or for something more testing, the inland walk of 14 miles from Sandwich to Dover which will take a full day. A shorter excursion would be the three-mile-round walk to the St Crispin Inn, a small attractive hotel in the pretty village of Worth.

From Sandwich it is best to travel south or inland since the towns and countryside to the north are less attractive. Deal, six miles south of Sandwich, is a fine old garrison town. The beach is lined with colourful hauled-out fishing boats and by the town centre stands Deal Castle, a 16th-century drum fort, built by Henry VIII and still armed with a battery of cannon. The Timeball Tower museum on the promenade is devoted to the study of time and telegraphy, and the pier is 300yd (274m) long and a boon to sea anglers.

Deal Castle is a real fort and somewhat grim, but Walmer Castle is far more appealing, part castle, part country house. Like Deal, Walmer Castle was built by Henry VIII as one of 20 forts put up to protect the coast from the French. These defences were entrusted to the Lord Warden of the Cinque Ports, and Walmer Castle became and remains the Warden's official residence. The present Warden is the Queen Mother. A visit to Walmer should allow time to enjoy the castle gardens with their great yew hedges and floral displays.

One should not be unkind about Dover, but the town centre is a traffic-jammed nightmare. That said, Dover makes every effort to entertain the visitor with a whole range of attractions, though the wise will head at once for Dover Castle, the 'Key to England', a splendidly preserved edifice, best seen from a mile offshore.

The castle stands on the site of an Iron Age fort and contains the remnants of a Roman lighthouse. The present castle was built by Henry II and completed in time for Henry's son, King John, to murder his rival and nephew, Arthur, in the dungeon. The coast of France is in plain sight from the ramparts and among the current attractions are a World of Espionage exhibition, a Battle of Waterloo model, and Hellfire Corner, a tour of the secret tunnels of the castle used as a command post in the Second World War. There is also the museum of the Queen's Regiment, and a great cannon presented to Henry VIII by the Emperor Charles V, 24ft (7.3m) long and known as Queen Elizabeth's Pocket Pistol.

**Queen Elizabeth's
Pocket Pistol,
Dover Castle**

After Dover has been explored there remains the cathedral city of Canterbury, 12 miles inland. Canterbury is the shopping centre hereabouts, with all the major chains in evidence as well as plenty of boutiques, galleries and antique shops in and around the pedestrian area near the cathedral.

This is the seat of the Primate of All England and contains the site of Becket's martyrdom, and the splendid tomb of Edward, eldest son of Edward III, known to history as the Black Prince. The prince's effigy lies on his tomb under a rail which bears his gauntlets, helmet, tabard and shield, but this is only one attraction in a building which is full of architectural splendour and many other memorials.

Canterbury also has a number of exhibitions and museums including a recreation of 14th-century England, The Canterbury Tales, which brings to life Chaucer's pilgrims and the stories they told each other on their journey. In Stour Street is Canterbury Heritage, a multi-media presentation of the city's history housed in an immaculately restored medieval building.

Sandwich and Deal, Dover, Walmer and Canterbury have the makings of a very full and pleasant weekend. And of course there is nothing to stop you coming back for more.

INFORMATION:

SANDWICH LIES AT THE JUNCTION OF THREE MAIN ROADS, THE A258 FROM DEAL, THE A256 FROM MARGATE AND RAMSGATE, AND THE A257 FROM CANTERBURY.

THE BELL HOTEL, SANDWICH, TEL. 0304 613388; THE ST CRISPIN INN, WORTH, TEL. 0304 612081. TIC (SANDWICH), TEL. 0304 613565; TIC (DEAL), TEL. 0304 369576.

35

Sherborne

—

Dorset is one of the prettiest of all the English counties. It has the Isle of Purbeck and the Dorset coast, the Thomas Hardy country around Dorchester, and a great number of small market towns and attractive villages.

Thanks to the steady expansion of the motorway network most of these are now in easy reach, but few places in Dorset are as charming or as interesting as the old town of Sherborne. Quite apart from having a lot to see within the town, Sherborne is a good touring centre for the country round about.

Sherborne is 50 miles from Bristol, 115 miles from Cardiff, 130 miles from London, and 145 miles from Birmingham.

According to John Aubrey, the 17th-century historian, Sir Walter Raleigh 'spoke broad Devon until his dying day', but Sir Walter's most enduring connection was with the town of Sherborne. He came there in 1592 after Elizabeth I granted him a lease on the 12th-century castle, and Sherborne remained his home for the rest of his life.

A man not unaccustomed to hardship, Sir Walter tried to withstand the rigours of the old castle with its damp and rats, but in 1594 he gave up the effort and decided to build a new one on the site of a former Tudor hunting lodge - and this castle remains, a far more successful venture.

Sherborne stands on the banks of the River Yeo and dates from the 8th century when a monastery was first built there. That monastic connection continues, for Sherborne is still an education centre with no less than 10 schools, including Sherborne public school. This occupies part of the former monastic buildings and has done so since the 16th century, when the abbey fell into secular hands after the Dissolution of the Monasteries.

The rest of the town is a pleasing mixture of architecture, part medieval, part Georgian, with lots of Victorian. Sherborne is a place to wander about in, full of narrow streets and cobbled corners, with the great abbey church as a centrepiece in the lower part of the town and the pretty town green serving a similar purpose at the top.

The green and the abbey are linked by Cheap Street, which is lined with shops of various kinds and leads down to Long Street and the Conduit. The Conduit, which much resembles a small market hall, was actually the monks' washing place. From there a narrow lane leads past the town museum and the abbey close to the Almshouse, a rambling late medieval building. This dates from 1437 and was built by the Bishop of Salisbury at the behest of Henry VI, for 'twelve poor feeble and ympotent old men and four old women', who apart from a roof over their heads were provided with a priest to pray for their souls, an office now performed by the Vicar of Sherborne.

The abbey at Sherborne is a magnificent building, even if the stone of the structure is prone to erosion and in constant need of repair. Even so, the exterior is splendid and the interior sublime. There are tombs and memorials and all the regimental colours of the Dorset Regiment, and spectacular fan-vaulting on the roof of the nave; while the tower supports the heaviest ring of eight bells in the world, the tenor bell a gift from Cardinal Wolsey in 1514.

As a base for a weekend in the town there is The Eastbury Hotel in Long Street. This is an early Georgian building erected in 1740, during the reign of George II. The hotel has retained most of the original features, including the library full of antiquarian books, while adding some modern ones like

The Conduit, Sherborne

the bar, which is decorated with Ronald Searle cartoons, and the restaurant which occupies a large conservatory overlooking the walled garden.

Those who choose to stay outside the town might prefer Plumber Manor at Sturminster Newton, 12 miles to the east down the A30 and A357. Plumber Manor is a Jacobean house, set beside the Develish trout stream, a tributary of the River Stour. It has a croquet lawn and tennis court and good food, and is an excellent touring base for the area.

First though, one must finish exploring Sherborne, where Sir Walter's second home and the Pageant Gardens remain to be inspected. Sir Walter was executed by James I and spent his last years in the Tower of London, while his home came into the possession of the Digbys. In 1625 Sir John Digby, the first Earl of Bristol, added the turrets which give this building a faintly Walt Disney look, and after the old castle was destroyed by Cromwell's troops in the Civil War, the new castle languished until Capability Brown was hired in the next century to work his wonders in the park and gardens.

Brown's additions include the lake, which now covers the original gardens laid out by Sir Walter, and 200 acres of woods and park which are open to visitors on every weekend from Easter to September. The Pageant Gardens, at the lower end of the town, were financed from the profits of the famous Sherborne Pageant, the first of its kind to be held in the town, with a cast of 1,000 players, organised for the townspeople by the wonderfully named Louis Napoleon Parker, a master at Sherborne School. This was the forerunner of all modern pageants.

Seven miles north of Sherborne lie the Cadburys of Somerset, two villages, North Cadbury and South Cadbury, set below the green mound called Cadbury Castle. Cadbury Castle, by repute the site of King Arthur's Camelot, is a vast Iron Age earthwork. From the top there are views over the Somerset Levels, towards the sharp distinctive spike of Glastonbury Tor and the Mendips beyond.

Getting to the top of Cadbury Castle is a good, one-hour walk along the footpath from the pretty village of South Cadbury. The village has a lot of stone cottages, each with a small flower-filled garden, and the church of St Thomas à Becket, which was built in the 14th century and has a fine contemporary wall-painting of a bishop, probably Becket himself, in his episcopal garments.

Heading south from Sherborne, 19 miles down the A352 brings the traveller to Dorchester, and shortly before that to Cerne Abbas. Dorchester is famous as the centre for the Thomas Hardy country and appears as Casterbridge in Hardy's books, where Sherborne features as Sherton Abbas; but Cerne Abbas is noted for its Giant, a large and decidedly phallic naked figure carved out of the turf on the hillside above the town.

The Giant is huge, 180ft (55m) high and 40ft (12m) across the shoulders, bearing a club 120ft (36.5m) long. It is almost certainly prehistoric and although preserved as a tourist attraction is still the centre of local legends, including one that says that women who want babies have only to sit on the Giant and their wish will soon be granted. See the Giant by all means but do not neglect Cerne Abbas village, which is full of fine half-timbered 16th-century houses.

Dorchester is a pleasant market town with Roman roots and a Thomas Hardy Museum, a court where the infamous Judge Jeffreys held one of his Bloody Assizes in 1688-9 after the Monmouth Rebellion, and lots of good pubs. Just south of Dorchester is another Iron Age hill-fort, and from Dorchester it is no distance south to Durdle Door and the beautiful Dorset coast, a grand place to be on a warm summer day.

On the way back to Sherborne from Dorchester, take the B3143 up the valley of the Piddle, which is always a talking point but a very pretty place, and the road through Puddletown, Piddlehinton and Piddletrenthide will eventually take you back again to Sherborne.

INFORMATION:

SHERBORNE LIES ON THE A30, YEOVIL TO SHAFTESBURY ROAD, FIVE MILES EAST OF YEOVIL.

THE EASTBURY MANOR, SHERBORNE, TEL. 0935 813131; PLUMBER MANOR, STURMINSTER NEWTON, TEL. 0258 72507; THE ANTELOPE HOTEL, SHERBORNE, TEL. 0935 812077. TIC (SHERBORNE), TEL. 0935 815341.

36

Southwold and the Suffolk Coast

—

The popular Aldeburgh aside, the coast of Suffolk is one of the less well known parts of England. Yet along this coastline there are some nice towns, magnificent churches, good beaches and wonderfully bracing sea air.

The centre for this weekend break is the former port of Southwold, a handsome town close to most of the attractions of this attractive county. Southwold is a good place to visit at any time of the year, but especially in the spring and autumn.

Southwold is 115 miles from London, and 180 miles from Birmingham.

Southwold is a Victorian seaside resort, where it would be no surprise to see small boys in sailor suits bowling hoops. Although a resort for over 100 years, Southwold remains unspoiled, and as with many Suffolk towns, the centre lies around a large and impressive church. Other attractions include a great lighthouse which towers above the rooftops of the town, and the charms of The Swan Hotel at the top of the High Street.

The Swan Hotel has been at the heart of Southwold life for centuries. The present building is a relative newcomer, being erected in 1660 after a fire the year before destroyed the old inn and much of the town. The hotel is a mixture of friendly bars and public rooms, with strikingly carved 18th-century door frames leading to the dining room and guest lounges.

If the interior of The Swan looks somewhat familiar to the first-time visitor that might be because the hotel and the town round about was used as the setting for the BBC television production of *David Copperfield*. Photos of the production decorate some of the hotel walls, combined with a collection of old prints.

The bars serve snacks - try the venison sausages and mash - while the food in the main dining room is based on local produce, especially fish. The hotel bakes its own bread and grows its own herbs, and has an excellent selection of wines in the cellars.

The Swan Hotel is right in the middle of Southwold and every part of the town lies within strolling distance. The town is almost an island, standing on a coastal knoll and surrounded by water on three sides - by the River Blyth to the south, by creeks and marshes which support a lot of birdlife to the west, and by the North Sea, which comes pounding in to a sand and shingle beach backed by a narrow promenade.

It is a short stroll to the sea across the green and along the promenade to the Sailors' Reading Room, which is now a maritime museum full of fascinating relics. This is just one of three museums in the town; there is a Lifeboat Museum on Gun Hill and the Southwold Museum on Bartholomew Green, which has paintings of the Battle of Sole Bay, a fight against the Dutch Navy which took place just offshore in 1672. Entrance to all these museums is free.

Then comes the bright white lighthouse and the church of St Edmund. There are so many fine churches in Suffolk that it is easy to suffer from nave fatigue, but the church at Southwold is rather special. It contains the 15th-century armoured figure of a soldier of the Wars of the Roses known as 'Southwold Jack'; also known as 'Jack o' the Clock' or 'Jack-smite-the-Clock', whose task was to toll the hours.

This figure is contemporaneous with the present church which was built in the 1460s in the pure Perpendicular style. Even people with a very low boredom threshold for churches will find St Edmund's worthwhile.

The town does have more secular pleasures. There are a number of good pubs, like the King's Head and the White Swan, and the Orwell Bookshop which can supply maps and guides to the local area; and when the streets of this charming town have been thoroughly explored there are walks across the common by the golf course or along the beach. There is also the river ferry or the footbridge to Walberswick.

Although Southwold itself is the main attraction hereabouts,

Walberswick is my special place along the Suffolk coast. It is very picturesque but far from twee, popular with artists who enjoy the clear North Sea light, and with birdwatchers who come to see the birds on the nature reserve at the head of the Blyth river estuary. Half a mile upstream lies the village of Blythburgh, which has yet another magnificent church and - he adds hastily - a very good pub, the White Hart.

Southwold is also a good touring centre. Thirteen miles to the north is the port of Lowestoft, which apart from offering the usual seaside joys of beach and bars, paddling pond and amusement park, is still - just - an active fishing port. It also offers a certain amount of evening entertainment, especially at the Spa Pavilion or the Marina Theatre.

A little to the north of Lowestoft is Somerleyton Hall, a Victorian mansion but famous locally for 12 acres of splendid garden and a maze, which is quite large enough to get lost in. Heading back towards Southwold the best route is via the little town of Bungay on the River Waveney. Bungay is a market town which, like Southwold somewhat earlier, was largely destroyed in a fire in 1688. The town was rebuilt in the following century in the Georgian style and as a result contains an exceptional number of fine buildings.

On the river a mile west of Bungay, at Earsham, is the home of the Otter Trust. The Otter Trust is a definite must on any visit to this part of Suffolk. There is a great collection of otters, for this is a major breeding and conservation centre, but the Trust also supports a herd of muntjac deer and a number of night herons.

Heading south along the coast the first place of note is the village of Dunwich, four miles along the beach, which is a tiny spot today and fast disappearing into the sea but was once the capital of East Anglia. Below Dunwich lies one of the finest bird reserves in Britain, Minsmere, which covers over 1,500 acres and supports a large bird population including many of the still rare avocet. Those who bring their field glasses will enjoy a visit to Minsmere, parts of which are open to the public from Minsmere Cliff. There are good walks through the reed beds and superb observation hides.

Further south still, along the A12 and the B1122, is the most famous place on the Suffolk coast, Aldeburgh, which would be worth a visit even without its long-standing connection with the late Benjamin Britten and Peter Pears, who lived there and began the Aldeburgh Festival in 1948. This has now expanded into a year-long round of concerts, music and the arts, with the original festival held in June and the Maltings Proms in August.

Other places well worth seeing in the hinterland behind the Suffolk coast include Framlingham, a quiet market town 20 miles south-west of Southwold, notable for a fine castle and a good historic hotel, The Crown, on Market Hill. The Crown was originally a 16th-century coaching inn but it seems even older than that, a place with low ceilings and creaking floors, where the stairway is built from interlocking beams and the bedrooms have four-posters. Apart from The Crown, Framlingham has many old houses lining winding narrow streets which lead up to the castle.

Spoonbill, Dunwich

From music festivals to nature reserves, Southwold has enough on its doorstep to fill any visit with interest. But for many, the greatest attraction of all will be a long invigorating walk by the sea.

INFORMATION:

SOUTHWOLD LIES ON THE A1095, EAST OF THE A12 FROM IPSWICH TO LOWESTOFT.

THE SWAN HOTEL, SOUTHWOLD, TEL. 0502 722186; THE WHITE LION HOTEL, ALDEBURGH, TEL. 0728 452720; THE CROWN HOTEL, FRAMLINGHAM, TEL. 0728 723521. TIC (SOUTHWOLD) TEL. 0502 724729; TIC (IPSWICH), TEL. 0473 258070.

Stamford

—

The Great North Road, now the more prosaic A1, is one of the famous highways of England. Dick Turpin used to ply his trade along it, stopping off to rest his horse and count his loot in one or other of the towns along the way, one of which was Stamford in Lincolnshire.

Stamford is one of the most attractive towns in England, a good centre for touring the bulb country of East Anglia but full of interest in its own right. It is a good place to visit at any time of year, but particularly in spring and summer, when the bulbs are out.

Stamford is 75 miles from Birmingham, 90 miles from London, 105 miles from Leeds, and 120 miles from Manchester.

To the first-time visitor Stamford is a surprise. It lies just a mile off the bustling A1, down in the valley of the River Welland, an enchanting lay-by in silver stone. The entire town was declared a conservation area in 1967 and proclaimed 'the finest stone-built town in England', a claim that it still makes good. Stamford is small but magnificent, the rooftops crowned and overtopped by a series of towers and spires from the many beautiful Gothic churches. The streets are lined with fine Georgian or medieval stone buildings, set off with flower-boxes and hanging baskets.

The town became a religous centre at the end of the Middle Ages, sheltering scholars who fled from the religious disputes causing turmoil in Oxford and Cambridge. During the Civil War Stamford was saved from total destruction by Lady Frances Wingfield who, claiming that they were related, persuaded Oliver Cromwell not to level the town after the Royalist garrison surrendered.

Stamford ought to be explored slowly and on foot, after checking in perhaps at The George Hotel, which lies at the bottom of St Martin's on the banks of the Welland. The George is not hard to find for the hotel signboard is suspended from the stout post that spans the street. This post was once the arm of the gibbet from which highwaymen were hanged. Further up St Martin's - which is a street, not a district - stands another local hostelry, the Garden House Hotel, which first opened at the beginning of the 19th century.

The George is a former coaching inn, one of the oldest and most frequented on the Great North Road, and the London Room and York Bar were originally waiting-rooms for the coach passengers while fresh horses were put into the shafts in the cobbled yard outside. Forty coaches a day put up at The George, 'twenty up and twenty down', and it remains a comfortable and hospitable place to stay. The hall contains a portrait of Stamford's most famous son, Daniel Lambert, the fattest man in England, who weighed over 52 stone (336kg) when he died in 1809 after years of dining rather too well at The George. His story is fleshed out at the Stamford Museum in Broad Street.

'The fattest man in England'

The George dates back to well before the turnpike days. It was the site of a commandery, or recruiting depot, for the legendary Knights of St John of Jerusalem. The mulberry tree in the garden dates from the reign of James I at the start of the 17th century, and part of the building was erected before that, by Lord Burghley who was Lord High Treasurer to Elizabeth I. His descendants, the Cecils, still live at Burghley House on the eastern edge of the town.

Stamford has medieval roots, though most of the old castle has long since disappeared and all that remains of the original town walls is the Bastion in St Peter's Street. The most striking architectural feature of the town today is the churches, all of them clustered around the town centre.

St George's church is medieval and associated with the Order of the Garter, since one of the first patrons was William de Bruges, the first Garter King of Arms, and a Royal Herald. One of the church windows is still decorated with Garters and medieval mottos. St John's is also medieval but smaller and has angel carvings in the roof; while St Martin's in the High Street was erected in 1430 and is a fine example of Perpendicular Gothic, with a pinnacled tower. St Martin's contains the tombs of the Cecil family, including that of William Cecil, the first Lord Burghley.

St Mary's church on St Mary's Hill was built and rebuilt between the 13th and 15th centuries; older still is St Leonard's Priory, which was founded by Benedictine monks around 1080. The almshouses, known as Browne's Hospital, in Broad Street were endowed by a local wool merchant, William Browne, in 1483. These now contain a museum of almshouse life, and there is some fine medieval glass in the chapel.

In spite of all these churches and old buildings Stamford should not be visualised as a museum piece. This is a lively market town, with a lot of good shopping around the High Street and a certain amount of evening entertainment. The Stamford Arts Centre in St Mary's Street offers a year-round programme of events and has an art gallery, and the Stamford Shakespeare Company puts on plays throughout the summer.

There is a series of waymarked walking trails around the town, most of them offering a theme, like Georgian or Victorian architecture, or a closer inspection of the town's chimneys. The TIC also has leaflets on longer rural rambles, some within Burghley Park and along the Welland.

After Stamford has been explored the time has come for a visit to Burghley House and a tour of the surrounding area. Burghley House is the largest and grandest of stately homes built in the Elizabethan Age, and since the founder, William Cecil, was obliged to entertain the Queen there on several occasions, no expense was spared to make the house comfortable. It was built between 1565 and 1587 and is a handsome, square building, crowned with turrets and cupolas and endowed with a great many windows.

The Deer Park was designed or redesigned by Capability Brown in the late 18th century, but the deer herd which inhabits the park dates back to 1562. The Deer Park is open to the public and offers both delightful walks and splendid views of the house. The park is the setting for the annual Burghley Horse Trials, and the Burghley sporting interests may be traced back to Lord Burghley, 6th Marquess of Exeter, who ran in the 1928 Olympics and appears as a character in the film *Chariots of Fire*, leaping over hurdles topped with full glasses of champagne.

Lord Burghley's trophies can be seen in the house, which contains a great quantity of treasures, including the finest collection of 17th-century Italian art in Britain, and works by Brueghel, Gainsborough, Kneller and Sir Thomas Lawrence. The house is open from April to early October and a guided tour takes in the Heaven Room, just one of 17 magnificently decorated State Rooms, with wonderful 17th-century wall and ceiling paintings by Verrio and carvings by Grinling Gibbons.

There is a porcelain collection and much fine furniture including four State Beds, one of them slept in by Queen Victoria. Lovers of history or admirers of Elizabeth I will also enjoy the displays of portraits and letters dating back to the first Lord Burghley, and the tour finishes in the Orangery, designed by Capability Brown to overlook the flower gardens. It now serves as a restaurant and coffee shop.

The countryside around Stamford will repay attention. To the west lies Rutland Water, where you can sail, fish for trout, or enjoy a host of other activities; to the east are the bulb fields of Lincolnshire around Spalding. Boston, on the edge of the Wash, is another bulb centre and a fine old port. Crowland Abbey lies in the fens a few miles to the east and Braceborough, two miles north-west of the town, is a picturesque village, once a spa and now a conservation area. Stamford is not to be missed, a place that must be included in any list of weekend breaks.

INFORMATION:

STAMFORD LIES JUST EAST OF THE A1 BETWEEN PETERBOROUGH AND GRANTHAM.

THE GEORGE, STAMFORD, TEL. 0780 55171; GARDEN HOUSE HOTEL, STAMFORD, TEL. 0780 63359. TIC (STAMFORD), TEL. 0780 55611.

38

Stonehouse and the Severn Valley

—

The village of Stonehouse in Gloucestershire is not particularly well known, but the setting is strategic. Stonehouse lies on the River Severn, close to the towns of Gloucester and Cheltenham, with a score of interesting and beautiful places round about, along the Severn Valley or on the southern slopes of the Cotswolds. Stonehouse is a four-seasons destination, with something to offer at every time of year.

Stonehouse is 30 miles from Bristol, 60 miles from Cardiff, 65 miles from Birmingham, and 110 miles from London.

The Stonehouse Court Hotel, the suggested base for the weekend, is just off the A419 a few miles west of Stroud, and the old manor house which contains it has close links with the history of the surrounding area. The manor is recorded in the Domesday Book and in the 13th century belonged to the Giffards, the last of whom was hanged, drawn and quartered in 1322 for plotting against King Edward II. Edward himself was later murdered in Berkeley Castle, a few miles to the south, and the estate passed to the Berkeleys for the annual payment of a rose.

The manor house, now a listed building, has gained a ghost or two and survived various fires with most of the fabric intact. The manor has been a hotel since 1983, but still has much of the original Tudor panelling.

Stonehouse Court is set in six acres of grounds and is a good centre for touring the Vale of Berkeley, the Severn Valley and the South Cotswolds. The only real problem is where to start.

To some extent, as always, it depends on the weather and the time of year. If the weather is poor, the places to visit are Gloucester and

Cheltenham.

Gloucester was a Roman town and has suffered from post-Second World War 'improvements', but nothing can detract from the glory of Gloucester Cathedral, which is in the Perpendicular style, with towers and spires which can be seen from miles away down the valley. The cathedral was once the abbey church and contains the tomb of Edward II and the Crécy window, with the blazonry of the knights who fought at

Regency Cheltenham

Crécy in 1346, the largest stained-glass window in the country. The nave has fan vaulting, and William the Conqueror ordered the compilation of the Domesday Book from the Abbey Chapter House.

Gloucester Cathedral warrants a prolonged browse, as do the narrow streets and alleys in the old part of the town, which are lined with small shops and boutiques and warm little pubs. The old docks are a conservation area and contain the National Waterways Museum.

Gloucester and Cheltenham are close together, but the two towns are quite different. Gloucester is medieval and cramped and full of small streets, while Cheltenham is an elegant spa, with boulevards and Regency buildings, open squares, parks full of flowers and trees, and some splendid plazas. Cheltenham has cinemas and theatres, supports a couple of arts festivals and is the birthplace of the composer Gustav Holst.

This is a town with a touch of class and some remarkably good shopping, especially around the Montpellier area, the original 18th-century spa. The Queen's Hotel dates back to 1838, and there are Regency buildings around the Imperial Gardens and Pittville Park, including the Pump Room which now contains a Gallery of Fashion.

Cheltenham is a fine town, but after the skies have cleared, it is time to go exploring. Those who like castles have a choice of two, starting with Sudeley Castle, seven miles to the north near Winchcombe. On the way there, leave the car and take a short stroll along Cleeve Hill, one of the highest points in the Cotswolds, with marvellous views over the Severn Valley.

Sudeley Castle was the home of Henry VIII's last and surviving wife, Catherine Parr, and although the original castle was destroyed in the Civil War, the ruins remain. The present castle was built in the 19th century and contains a collection of paintings by Van Dyck, Rubens and Turner. Queen Catherine is buried in the chapel, and there are no less than eight separate gardens, including the formal Queen's Garden which is surrounded by thick yew hedges.

The other castle is Berkeley, some distance to the south. To get there involves a beautiful drive along the southern slopes of the Cotswolds, through places made famous by Laurie Lee in his book *Cider with Rosie*, like the village of Slad. There are lots of pretty places, including Prinknash Abbey and the lovely little wool town of Painswick.

Prinknash, off the A46, is home for a community of monks. The park still contains the old abbey, once a hunting lodge for Henry VIII and the abbots of Gloucester. There is also the new abbey, a famous and excellent pottery, and Prinknash Bird Park, which has some exotic birds and a few animals.

If Prinknash is entertaining, Painswick is a gem. It is called 'The Queen of the Cotswolds', and while that title might be disputed, Painswick is undoubtedly very lovely; a tight, silver-stone town with the most splendid church, where the tombs in the churchyard are set off by a collection of yews. To see the yew trees of Painswick is enough to justify a visit, especially in mid-summer when the bright green of the new growth is a wonderful sight.

The inside of Painswick church is something else to see. The tapestry kneelers are real works of art, the Lady Chapel dates from 1377 and there are carvings on the pillars made by Parliamentary soldiers besieged in the church in 1643.

Painswick also has the Falcon Hotel, which dates back to 1544 and has the oldest bowling green in the country. Westhaven House in the main street is the oldest building in England to house a post office, while other attractions include the six acres of the 17th- and 18th-century Rococo Garden, and several good pubs. A morning in Cheltenham and Gloucester followed by a visit to Sudeley and Painswick would make the perfect day.

Berkeley Castle, 15 miles south-west of Stonehouse, is the place where Edward II was murdered with a red-hot poker in a manner better imagined than described. The Berkeley family still live in the castle as they have done since the 12th century, and their home is a classic medieval stronghold. It has a drum keep dating from 1153, surrounded by the walls breached by Cromwell's cannon in 1645. The interior of the castle is pure medieval, and includes the King's Chamber where Edward II was imprisoned and done to death. All the rooms are full of paintings and furniture, armour and banners, collected during the family's long residence.

Seven miles north of Berkeley, just off the A38, lies the Wildfowl and Wetlands Trust at Slimbridge, created in 1946 by the late Sir Peter Scott, an ardent protector of wildlife, especially birds. Slimbridge is another good reason for a weekend hereabouts, a marvellous place to pass an hour or two in any season of the year.

Slimbridge plays host to hundreds of geese, ducks and waders, and contains a resident population of some 7,000 birds of 200 different kinds, all of which can easily be seen from the hides and walkways through the ponds.

A weekend around Stonehouse has a great deal to offer. Minchinhampton and Stroud are worth a brief visit; there is walking and great views on Birdlip Hill, east of Gloucester, and regular meetings at Cheltenham Racecourse, with the contrasting countryside of the Cotswolds and the Severn Valley as the background to it all.

INFORMATION:

STONEHOUSE LIES ON THE A419 BETWEEN STROUD AND JUNCTION 13 ON THE M5 BETWEEN GLOUCESTER AND BRISTOL.

STONEHOUSE COURT HOTEL, STONEHOUSE, TEL. 045382 5155; THE FALCON HOTEL, PAINSWICK, TEL. 0452 812189; HOTEL DE LA BERE, SOUTHAM, CHELTENHAM, TEL. 0242 237771; THE GREENWAY HOTEL, SHURDINGTON, CHELTENHAM, TEL. 0242 862352. TIC (GLOUCESTER), TEL. 0452 421188; TIC (CHELTENHAM), TEL. 0242 522878.

39

Ullswater and the Northern Lakes

—

Although this book tends towards the less well known but always beautiful parts of Britain, there has to be the odd exception. One of these is the Lake District of Cumbria, such a wonderful place to visit that no tour of Britain can really leave it out; with one small caveat - maybe two.

The first is to avoid the Lake District in July and August. The reader will thank me for that advice and the locals will thank the reader for taking it. My vote is for the early spring or autumn when the crowds are smaller. The two visits for this book were made at the end of October and early December, and the weather on both occasions was glorious.

The second suggestion is to avoid Windermere, and head north beyond Grasmere to Ullswater and the northern lakes, where the crowds are smaller and the scenery every bit as fine.

Watermillock on Ullswater is 75 miles from Newcastle, 95 miles from Manchester, 105 miles from Leeds, and 130 miles from Edinburgh or Glasgow.

The northern lakes begin at Ambleside, that attractive village at the foot of the steep narrow road that runs down from the top of the Kirkstone Pass. These northern lakes, Ullswater, Grasmere, Derwent Water, Bassenthwaite, Buttermere and the rest, lie on either side of the Cumbrian Mountains, around the town of Keswick, roughly between Penrith and Cockermouth.

The Lake District, north or south, is walking country. On any weekend the car parks and lay-bys will be full of empty cars, while the occupants are out on the nearby fells. This is serious walking country, with very changeable weather, so good boots, sensible clothing and a well-marked trail are advisable for anyone who is not already a fully experienced hill-walker.

As a base for this weekend I propose Ullswater and the Leeming House hotel at Watermillock, which has 20 acres of gardens, a room stocked with information on what to do in the area, and a library full of books to while away a wet day. The daffodils in these gardens inspired Wordsworth's famous poem and are certainly an inspiring sight in the spring.

The Lake District is wonderfully compact and full of glorious sights, so on a first visit, any wise traveller will opt for a ride around some of the lakes, a tramp on the fells and a cruise on one of the lake steamers or

Lake cruises

launches. In the winter months this may mean a cruise on Windermere, but for much of the year there are half-day or one-hour trips down most of the major lakes.

People argue happily about the finest lakes and the finest views, but the following tour will take in some of the best. From Watermillock, take the road south through Glenridding and Patterdale. On the way look west, for views to Helvellyn and Grisedale. There are good walks to the top of Helvellyn (3,116ft/949m) and the TIC at Glenridding will be able to advise on routes and times. The jumbled crags west of Patterdale are glorious to behold and the road climbs up to the top of the Kirkstone Pass, from where there are more views down to Windermere.

At the top of the pass stands a medieval inn, dating from the late 15th century and still a refuge for walkers on the fells. A coffee or a bowl of soup here is a good idea before taking that narrow, steep and winding road which plunges down to Ambleside.

Ambleside, Grasmere and Rydal Water are the centres for the Wordsworth industry. Wordsworth himself declared that Grasmere was 'the loveliest spot that man hath ever found', and here is Dove Cottage where he and his sister Dorothy used to live and entertain their friends.

Wordsworth taught at the village school which is now the Gingerbread Shop, and Grasmere gingerbread remains one of the toothsome local attractions. That apart, all these places are quite remarkably pretty and the best way to see them is to park - a near impossible task in summer - and take an hour out of the car to stroll through the villages, visit the Grasmere and Wordsworth Museum and enjoy lunch in one of the local hotels or pubs.

Ambleside tends to be full of people even in the winter months, but has to be seen, if only for the tiny 17th-century Bridge House over the Stock Ghyll which was built as a summerhouse for the local landowner and is now a National Trust Information Centre. The church of St Mary at Ambleside has a steeple 120ft (37m) high and celebrates the annual rush-bearing ceremony on the first Saturday in July, a relic of the time when most churches were carpeted with rushes against the muddy boots of the congregation.

A good hotel here is Michael's Nook at Grasmere which is full of antiques and patrolled by a couple of massive and amiable Great Danes, which are bred by the owner and win all the prizes at the local dog shows. The hotel has good views over the surrounding fells and is very popular with walkers.

From here take the route up Thirlmere, turning onto the road on the west of the lake for views across it to Helvellyn. It is possible to climb Helvellyn from this side and the track up to the summit can easily be traced across the side of the mountain, though the trip up and down would take a reasonably fit walker at least half a day.

After returning to the main A591 head north to Keswick at the head of Derwent Water. Keswick is recognised as the capital of the northern lakes and sights to see include the Castlerigg Stone Circle on a hill to the east of the town; and there are cruises on Derwent Water. Keswick too had its share of poets, for Coleridge, Shelley and Robert Southey lived here in the early years of the last century.

The Town Trail takes in the poets' homes and many of Keswick's craft shops and ateliers, not forgetting the Cumberland Pencil Museum. There are good walks along the shore of the lake, including a one-and-a-half-mile stroll to Friar's Crag, where the views over the lake and fells are among the best in the District. There are more fine views from the summit of Skiddaw (3,054ft/930m), which lies just north of the town. There is a good, stiff but popular walk up Skiddaw from the A591.

From Keswick take the A66 north and west along the shores of Bassenthwaite Lake to the junction with the B5292, just east of Cockermouth. Turn south there through the vale to Buttermere and Crummock Water, which are practically one stretch of water, set in the most beautiful Lakeland scenery. There is excellent fell-walking around here with steep but short walks up Red Pike (2,479ft/755m) or along the ridge of Buttermere Fell (2,417ft-2,473ft/736m-753m). Buttermere and most of the lake shore are now owned by the National Trust and there are guided walks around the area from the car park.

Close to Keswick lies Buttermere, in an area full of famous Lakeland places, with fells like Hay Stacks just to the south, the 120ft (37m) drop of the Scale Force waterfall, and the Honister Pass to the east which runs between the fells towards Borrowdale and Keswick. From Keswick there is a fine scenic route through the northern fells to Troutbeck, from where the A5091 leads south across the hills and back to Ullswater.

This is simply a small sample of all the glories the Lake District has to offer. Anyone who spends a weekend here, stopping to look at the sights and take a walk or two, will certainly have a wonderful time and leave determined to come back again.

INFORMATION:

WATERMILLOCK LIES ON THE A592 FROM PENRITH TO WINDERMERE.

LEEMING HOUSE, WATERMILLOCK, TEL. 07684 86622; MICHAEL'S NOOK, GRASMERE, TEL. 05394 35496. TIC (ULLSWATER), TEL. 07684 82414; TIC (KESWICK), TEL. 07687 72645.

40

Winsford and Exmoor

—

Exmoor is a beautiful and remote part of the West Country, a rolling open heath seamed with steep-sided forest valleys, dotted with small red-stone villages and well supplied with minor roads. Exmoor is uncrowded even in the heart of summer but is best visited in the spring, when the bluebells and snowdrops are out, or in early autumn, from mid-September to the end of October, when the leaf change makes the deep forested valleys a russet-red backdrop to the purple heather on the moor.

Winsford is 75 miles from Bristol, 115 miles from Cardiff, and 155 miles from Birmingham.

Exmoor is divided between two counties and straddles the boundary between North Devon and the coast of West Somerset. Although the North Devon side has its attractions, this weekend concentrates on the Exmoor National Park and the places that lie within Somerset, either along the coast or on the moor itself. As you will see, this still gives the visitor plenty of scope.

The suggested base for this weekend is the Royal Oak Inn at Winsford, a tiny village in the middle of Exmoor. The Royal Oak is a thatched, 12th-century medieval inn, converted into a small but very comfortable hotel, with a large hunting mural on the wall of the residents' lounge and good food in the bar or the restaurant.

The hotel is popular with walkers and shooting parties, and the proprietor is full of information about the area and provides a map illustrating all the places of interest in the countryside roundabout.

Pretty Winsford is an oasis of calm. Wander around the village in the early evening or first thing in the morning and the only sound is the voices from the pub garden or the bleating of sheep on the hill.

Back in 1909 the writer W.H.Hudson wrote that Winsford offered 'fragrant, cool, grey green, immemorial peace - second to no English village in beauty, with running waters, stone and thatched cottages, a hoary church tower.' Not much has changed in Winsford in the intervening years.

One good walk from Winsford is up the hill behind the village, a half-day climb to the 1,704ft (519m) height of Dunkery Beacon, which lies at the heart of the moor and has views over the surrounding countryside and across the Bristol Channel. Exmoor ponies and red deer can be found on the open moor, while in the river valley of the Exe, which rises on Exmoor, wagtails run about among the rocks and kingfishers flash past between patches of sun and shadow.

The red deer - Britain's largest wild animal - is one of the glories of Exmoor and the Exmoor herd is the largest outside Scotland. The 'rut' or mating season begins in early autumn when the roaring of the stags can be heard for miles. By autumn too the foals of the Exmoor pony herd are about, grazing beside the road or beginning to drift into the shelter of the valleys. The ponies are not truly wild - they all belong to someone - and the two main herds can be seen at Haddon Hill and near Larkbarrow.

In late summer the mix of purple heather and golden gorse creates a great carpet of colour across the hills above the green valleys and the turning woodland leaf; but Exmoor supports more than a thousand different plant varieties in a range of habitat from heath to coastal headland. Full details of local plant and animal life can be found at the various Park Visitors' Centres.

Other animals to look out for include the badger and the fox. Among the birds that flourish on the heaths of Exmoor are the merlin and peregrine falcon; green and spotted woodpeckers can be found in the valleys, while the reservoir and lake at Clatworthy and Wimbleball attract the water rail, the grebe and various species of duck and geese. A good field guide and a pair of binoculars would be useful.

Much of Exmoor is taken up by the 265 square miles of the Exmoor National Park and a good place to start a weekend in the area is with a

Red deer, Exmoor

visit to the Park headquarters at Dulverton, six miles south of Winsford. On the way there one essential diversion is to Tarr Steps, on the River Barle. Tarr Steps is a beauty spot famous for its ancient clapper bridge, which is simply a series of great stone slabs laid low across the river, underwater in wintertime when the river rises but far too heavy and solid to be swept away in the spring floods. Those who want to walk to Tarr Steps and linger must park halfway down the hill; those who fancy only a quick look can drive down and up again.

Exmoor is ideal for car touring, with plenty of parking places beside the moorland roads. One good route which gives an overview of the entire area is the B3223, which can be picked up just west of Winsford and followed north to Simonsbath and then on to the coast; or you can travel east along the B3224 (from where it meets the B3223) to Exford and Wheddon Cross. All these are pretty places, but the big attraction is the breezy views from either side of the road as you journey across the moor.

Walking is the great activity on Exmoor. There are waymarked footpaths everywhere; the National Park offices run a daily series of guided walks throughout the summer months, and most of the shops and Tourist Information Centres sell walking books and guides. Pony-trekking is also available from most of the towns and villages, and other sports include fishing for salmon on the Exe, Barle and East Lyn rivers.

Those who enjoy sightseeing are spoiled for choice on Exmoor. Among the many places to visit is Dulverton, a charming and ancient town. Before the Conquest it belonged to Harold, Earl of Wessex (later King Harold), who was killed by the Normans on Senlac Hill at the Battle of Hastings. Dulverton has a lot of pubs, including the Carnavon Arms and the Anchor Inn.

Sir Francis Drake is said to have lived at Sydenham Hall and Dulverton is the place where Lorna Doone, one of the great literary characters of Exmoor, first set eyes on her lover, John Ridd. Dulverton is a lively town, which hosts a carnival on the first Saturday in October.

The best way to see and enjoy Exmoor is to wander about on foot or by car; mountain-biking is popular but the hills are very steep. From Winsford it is a short drive north to one of the most picturesque places hereabouts, the village of Dunster and Dunster Castle, home of the Luttrell family.

Dunster is a medieval village and has all the essential medieval trappings. Apart from the castle there is a church, a mill, a dovecote, a packhorse bridge and the Luttrell Arms Hotel, which was once the residence of the local abbot. The streets are lined with red-stone houses, draped with flowers and hanging baskets.

The centrepiece of the village is the castle, which was built soon after the Norman Conquest, added to over the centuries, and was the home of the Luttrells for 600 years until they handed it over to the National Trust in 1976. Dunster Park, which surrounds the castle, is ideal for picnics and rambles and there is a good two-hour walk from the village to the top of Withycombe Hill, from where there are views to the Quantocks (once the stamping ground of the poets Wordsworth and Coleridge) and Wales.

If the moors are the main attraction, the north coast of Somerset is an added bonus. Minehead is the principal town, though too full of tourists, but Blue Anchor and Blue Anchor Bay are well worth a visit. West of here lies the village of Porlock and the little fishing port of Porlock Weir, which is still very beautiful, with a good pub and a pebble beach.

West of Porlock, south of the A39 road and just before the Devon border, lies the village of Oare and Lorna Doone Country. R.D.Blackmore, the author of *Lorna Doone*, lived in Oare where his father was the vicar, and the village church features in the book as the place where Lorna gets married and is shot by the villainous Carver Doone. Apart from the church there is very little to see in Oare, no pub, no post office and only 50 residents, but the 'Doone Country' to the south is stunning.

Exmoor is full of attractions, man-made or natural, but top of the list must be the clear air, the wonderful views and the general peace and quiet. It all adds up to a great weekend.

INFORMATION:

WINSFORD LIES NORTH-WEST OF THE VILLAGE OF EXTON ON THE A396 FROM TIVERTON TO DUNSTER.

THE ROYAL OAK INN, WINSFORD, TEL. 0643 85455; THE LUTTRELL ARMS, DUNSTER, TEL. 0643 821555. TIC (MINEHEAD), TEL. 0643 702624; TIC (LYNTON), TEL. 0598 52225.